Back to the Afterl...

Bernie Kastner

Back to the Afterlife

Uncovering the Mysteries
of What Happens to Us Next

RVP Press

New York

RVP Publishers Inc.
95 Morton Street, Ground Floor
New York, NY 10014

RVP Press, New York

© 2013 Bernie Kastner / RVP Publishers Inc., New York

RVP Press™ is an imprint of RVP Publishers Inc., New York
The RVP Publishers logo is a registered trademark of RVP Publishers Inc., New York

Library of Congress Control Number: 2013947682

ISBN 978 1 61861 312 7

www.rvppress.com

To My Father, Irving Kastner, of blessed memory

Contents

Introduction

*"The living can no more understand the afterlife
than a blind man can understand color."*
—*Tracey R. Rich*

L IFE AFTER DEATH: one of humanity's great enigmas. It preoc-
cupies some, terrifies some, and motivates some, for better
or for worse. But most of all, it baffles. How different might
our lives be if we truly grasped what lies beyond this life? Would we
still fear death if the afterlife wasn't concealed in darkness, cloaked
in mystery; its secrets guarded by mystics, priests and rabbis? What
if each of us could grasp, even fractionally, what lies in the great
void beyond, after we take our last breath and close our eyes for the
last time?

These are the questions I began to ask myself following the
death of my precious 19-year-old son, Gedalia, after a short but
devastating illness. The suffering my family experienced was nearly
intolerable. The loss of a child, as any grieving parent could tell
you, cannot be adequately expressed in words. But as I dealt with

this crippling blow, I began to wonder how much of my suffering was justified. Had I truly lost my son, or had he simply moved onto another dimension, a natural step along his infinite journey in the universe? Was he really looking down on me from a better place?

It may seem futile to even attempt to understand the afterlife. After all, who can tell us with any certainty about a place from which there is apparently no return? Yet the literature on this ostensibly unknowable topic is vast, as documented in my first book, *Understanding the Afterlife in This Life* (Devora, 2007). The idea that the consciousness or soul of a being continues after physical death occurs is nearly universal to all those who believe in a spiritual realm. From the ancient Egyptians to the ancient Greeks, from the Zoroastrians to the Norse, from Jews to Christians and Muslims, Hindus, Sikhs and Buddhists to Seventh-day Adventists—all are bonded by their belief that the soul does continue on its journey following death.

Going through religious texts, I discovered that all these races and religions from all parts of the world were bonded by common threads, elements of an afterlife that were eerily similar. Could it be coincidence, or is there something factual, a truth that is universal?

Buddhist and Brahminical wisdom endorse metempsychosis, the transmigration of the soul into a new body after death; Platonists defined the body as a "prison" from which the soul escaped; and Hindus believe that the soul is immortal and imperishable, reincarnating to overcome its inconsistencies and blemishes. All of this and more are shared by the Jewish faith with the concept of a *neshama*—a kind of spiritual intelligence separate from the body. It is mentioned for the first time early on in *Genesis* (2:7) where it is written: "Then the Lord God formed the man of dust of the ground, and breathed into his nostrils the breath of life; and the man became a living soul."

And why shouldn't this concept be found universally if it is not a universal truth? Wouldn't one expect a synchronicity of beliefs if an "afterlife" does exist?

It occurs to me that universal truths are embedded in the soul, no matter what race or religion you are born into. It is a collective truth, and it accounts for the similarity in our beliefs. We gravitate toward the truth naturally.

And there may be a reason for this. According to Jewish belief, before we are born we already possess all the knowledge of the Torah and the universe. But prior to entering this world, an angel is said to touch our upper lips, creating an indentation and causing us to forget all of truths we have learned. These truths are not forgotten entirely, however. When we relearn these truths in our lives, they "ring true" because they are "remembered" and "recognized." Is there not something like this in our deep sense that an afterlife awaits us?

History is replete with great minds that agree—there are mystical truths that exist beyond our comprehension. One of them, Albert Einstein, proclaimed: "That which is impenetrable to us really exists. Behind the secrets of nature remains something subtle, intangible, and inexplicable."

When Einstein said this, do you suppose he, with all his scientific logic, did not suspect that life beyond this earthly existence was possible?

Others also agree. One of the most fascinating guidebooks on the afterlife is the Jewish mystical text, the Zohar, better known as the Kabala. The Zohar has become fashionable of late in celebrity circles, but for centuries its ancient mystical teachings have been entrusted to the most brilliant of Jewish students and scholars because of its complicated and esoteric nature. In this book, I will attempt to share some of the information I have gleaned from the Zohar on this topic. I take a deeper look into what specific steps we are destined to take in the next world and explain what can we do in our current lives to help make that road a better one on which to travel.

I wanted to give a very clear picture of what we will feel and what we will experience, stage-by-stage, as we move along life's continuum. Those who have had a near-death experience (NDE) were only able to go so far—all have reported a roadblock beyond which is the point of "no return." At that juncture they are told that they are not yet ready to go beyond the roadblock and that they must return to this world to complete certain tasks. That's the theme of my second book, *Masa El Ha'or* (*Journey to the Light*, Hebrew, Zmanma 2010), a children's story.

In a very small number of cases, a choice is actually presented—to proceed beyond the roadblock or to go back to this life. In this book, we move beyond that roadblock.

We look at the "transition" (a term I prefer to "death") from this life to the next. Using kabalistic and other sources in Jewish philosophy, and even science, we explore the route a soul takes from the period 30 days before transitioning, through the actual transition, and the various stations it reaches along its forward journey.

By uncovering territory previously unknown to the majority of us, lessons can be drawn not only about what we can expect in the life to come, but also give a new perspective on the lives we're living today. Though some sections of the path may be unsettling, it is my hope that giving exposure to this great transition from life to afterlife will ultimately bring hope and comfort, dispel the fear of the unknown and offer illumination to those grappling with the great beyond.

CHAPTER ONE

A Vision of the Afterlife

"Don't worry about the world coming to an end today.
It's already tomorrow in Australia."
—*Charles Schulz*

IT'S NOT SURPRISING that most people have tremendous anxiety about the prospect of dying. In *The American Heritage Dictionary*, "death" is defined as an end, a termination of activity, a point of no return. Further, it states that it is a loss or absence of spiritual life. That sounds awful, doesn't it? Moreover, it is not correct! We do not so much die as "transition" to another plane. When we transition, it is not the end, nor is it a point of no return. And it is certainly not without spirituality. Rather, we, our souls, are in a process of changing from one form and place to another. We are moving along, constantly learning, and even have additional chances to return to this world in another incarnation (also referred to in this text as a *gilgul*).

Yes, the Jewish faith believes in reincarnation—but not only reincarnation. We believe in heaven, purgatory, guardian angels and even ghosts. Does this surprise you? Well, it might, because so little of what we learn in school is connected to what awaits us in the afterlife. But all these concepts that we believe in are not as threatening as you might imagine. Purgatory, non-threatening? Well, in a sense, yes. Our general lack of knowledge about the afterlife is ultimately more anxiety-inducing than the knowledge itself.

As we begin to explore the afterworld, discard your preconceived notions of what heaven, hell, devils and angels are. The world that awaits us functions according to the laws of God, not modern-day movie producers. And the Kabala is one of our most trusted sources for delving into this realm of spiritual existence.

When we talk about Kabala we are referring to Torah mysticism authored by the great scholar Rabbi Shimon bar Yochai (80–160 CE). Bar Yochai wrote the Zohar (Book of Splendor), which forms the basis of Kabala (Jewish Mysticism). Rabbi Yitzchak Luria (1534–1572), also known as "The Ari," was a foremost rabbi and Jewish mystic in the community of Safed. He is considered the father of contemporary Kabala and published the Zohar for the first time in 1558. His disciples compiled his oral teachings into writing. The main popularizer of Luria's ideas was Rabbi Chaim Vital, also a sixteenth-century kabalist and Torah scholar.

So why is all the information on the afterlife relegated to an esoteric text, and not explicitly revealed to us in the Torah?

According to Rabbi Louis Jacobs (1920–2006), a leading writer and thinker on Judaism from England, "One of the most remarkable features of Jewish belief in the Hereafter is the absence of any kind of definite information in the Bible. Though a detailed account of the afterlife may not be found in the Hebrew Scriptures, there are certainly clues that show that there was a concept of life after death. The account of Saul and the medium at Endor in the first book of

Samuel shows that there was a concept of the continued existence of Samuel and other individuals after death."

In the Talmud we have numerous sources pointing to the existence of an afterlife. In the Talmud Yerushalmi (Mishna Yevamot 16:3) it states: "For three days after passing away, the spirit hovers over the body... the deceased knows everything that is said in front of him." In Tractate Brachot (18b) there is reference to souls that converse between themselves after death. In Ketubot (103a) we learn about Rabbi Yehuda Hanassi (a second-century Jewish leader who compiled the Mishnah, the first major written text of Jewish oral traditions) who would visit his home every Sabbath eve after his passing. In Taanit (23b) we are introduced to a Torah scholar who would help out his son after his passing.

Jacobs continues: "Some modern Jews clearly have no use for any doctrine of a Hereafter and, oddly enough, this includes some religious Jews. Many regard Judaism as a religion that focuses on the here-and-now and some consider the entire notion of the afterlife irrelevant." In fact, the first translations from the Hebrew of Jewish classic medieval texts on the afterlife were done by rationalists who were ashamed to publish texts that could be perceived as mere superstition.

Yet there are many who find the notion to be very relevant. Part of the strength of the doctrine of resurrection in Jewish theology is that it is stressed in Talmudic literature, in Jewish liturgical texts, in Jewish burial ceremonies and in medieval Jewish discussions.

I am sympathetic to this view. To me, the afterlife is a central notion of Jewish belief that could help inform the way we live our lives. So we will be visiting up close the various regions of the afterlife, from the tunnel at the Cave of the Patriarchs to *Gan Eden*, *gehinom*, the divine temples and more.

But ultimately, how can we know what exists in the afterlife? It is in some ways the "great unknown"—a realm from which no man can return to give testimony. Although it seems a futile task to try to understand such an impenetrable subject, there are some scientific methodologies that have succeeded in shedding light on life beyond this life, giving credence in many instances to the ancient beliefs of religious traditions.

Over the years, bodies of information have been gathered by both scientific and esoteric means. Past life regressions carried out by hypnotherapists, near-death experiences, unusual and bizarre occurrences, dreams and out-of-body experiences have all shed light, however slight, on the world beyond. Through the personal experiences of the people involved, data began to be compiled. Comparisons by researchers, hypnotists, psychotherapists, physicians, philosophers and academics were then made among and between accounts and information that began to surface. As a result, articles, books, organizations, clubs, and of course major motion pictures, were devoured by the public. There are still those who remain skeptical about anything they can't see with their own eyes, but there are millions of others who are utterly fascinated with the prospect that there is something out there beyond the here and now.

This prospect not only gives people hope by reassuring many that the end of our lives is not necessarily the end of our journey, but it also offers a new way of looking at our time here on earth. By getting a sense of what the afterlife holds, and our souls' purpose here on earth and beyond, we can apply this knowledge to the management of our lives.

So just how does one develop an intimate knowledge of the afterlife? After all, there is no shortage of sources. My journey into the subject is one that took me on a long and circuitous path. I left no stone unturned, and never dismissed anything outright. Only once I had studied all the sources I could get my hands on did a clear and true vision finally begin to materialize.

I began with a series of books written by secular thinkers, doctors and scientists. For instance, *More Lives Than One? The Evidence of the Remarkable Bloxham Tapes* by Jeffrey Iverson (1976) describes how a professional hypnotherapist, Arnall Bloxham, over a period of time hypnotized a Welsh housewife, Jane Evans, and obtained very detailed accounts of six of her previous lives during the past 2000 years. Jeffrey Iverson, a television producer, researched the detail of Evans' recalled lives, and found tremendous factual data to indicate that her recollections were founded on fact.

In *Reliving Past Lives* (1979), Helen Wambach, a psychologist and clinical psychiatrist, developed a hypnotic technique by which she was able to regress her subjects back to previous lives. Over a period of 12 years, in a carefully designed project, she hypnotically regressed more than 1000 subjects. Choosing specific time periods within an overall span of 4000 years she asked her subjects questions about their appearance, sex, clothing, lifestyle and feelings at the moment of death for each specific incarnation. Each subject was given a post-hypnotic suggestion that enabled him or her to fill out a data sheet with precise details for each incarnation following the session.

In *Other Selves, Other Lives, A Jungian Psychotherapist Discovers Past Lives* (1987), Roger J. Woolger explores the connection between past life illness and current life fitness—both emotional and physical.

Mary Davies in *The Journey: A Spiritual Autobiography Spanning Two Thousand Years* (1999) used six of her own past lives and her present life to weave a fascinating account of how the human soul evolves over the centuries, making mistakes and learning valuable lessons, and how the continuing process is a spiritual journey to the Cosmic Source of Divine Love.

And *Journey of Souls* (1994) by Michael Newton describes processes of hypnotic regression whereby people recall accounts of their past lives. What is exceptional about Newton's books, among the many others out there, is that it is the first book in which, through hypnosis, individuals are urged to recall otherwise lost memories of the periods *between* former incarnations on earth—providing accounts from 29 individual cases. *Journey of Souls* uniquely provides detailed accounts of the processes of death and the soul's progression through the afterlife.

I have personally found the empirical evidence brought to light by Newton to be the most enlightening for several compelling reasons. Of all the researchers I've studied, Newton's strictly secular and scientific research was surprisingly the most similar to the ancient scriptures of the kabalistic sages. He was also the first to make the bold move of quantifying steps along the continuum of life after we leave this world.

Newton, an American psychotherapist and hypnotherapist in private practice, devoted his energies toward helping people access their higher spiritual selves through the development of his own age-regression technique. He discovered it was possible to take his clients beyond their past-life experiences to uncover a more meaningful soul existence between lives. He is considered to be a pioneer in uncovering the mysteries about life in the spirit world, first reported in his best-selling book *Journey of Souls*, which has been translated into 10 languages. In 1998 he received the annual award for the "Most Unique Contribution" in bridging mind, body, and spirit from the National Association of Transpersonal Hypnotherapists. Together with his second best-selling book *Destiny of Souls*, his books have sold over one million copies.

I found pieces in his research that were missing from the esoteric kabalistic texts I studied, yet noticed that he had details recorded on the afterlife that uncannily mirrored the kabala. There were, of course, also pieces of his research that were not mentioned in any of the texts I reviewed and vice versa, but overall, what I saw before me was a truly amazing opportunity to bring together the various and sundry pieces of this enigmatic puzzle to create a fuller picture: a beautiful symbiosis of mysticism and science that will produce an enriching and more complete map of the journey we take after leaving this world.

Toward that end, I took the between-lives accounts reported by Newton, compared them to what we know from our kabalistic texts, and came up with a combined step-by-step virtual tour of what transpires in the afterlife. This includes our emotions, thoughts, feelings, memories, the people we meet and associate with, reviewing our past lives and the decisions we made, considering how we would go about our lives if given another opportunity, and some of the unpleasant moments as well.

As you read on you will become familiar with the 46 steps delineated on this virtual tour. Twenty-five of these steps are described by Newton's subjects; 21 are from Judaic sources. There are steps that overlap as well and are described by both sources. It is especially noteworthy to mention here that these steps apply to both Jewish souls and to the souls of righteous gentiles.

For some with an even greater curiosity, "life between lives" regression is an opportunity to get a clearer vision of one's soul. This kind of hypnotically induced regression helps people find answers to questions, and can bring a deep sense of meaning. In a session three to five hours in length, one typically revisits the course of our journey and analyzes actions and choices we have made in our previous lifetimes. Through this process, one can come to recognize the unique contributions that only you can make in this life.

In this process, one is progressed in time through the death experience of a previous life and into the spirit realm of life between lives. A number of lasting impressions and important information may arise as an outcome of this process, such as understanding our soul's purpose, special gifts we have in this lifetime, why we chose our present body and family, and better insight into life's challenges. Imagine how different our lives would be with this absolute knowledge.

In Newton's between-lives research, people with different backgrounds and religious beliefs had many similar experiences in their travels through the afterworld. However, memories can be blocked during regression, and therefore not every memory of a subject under hypnosis will be available. Moreover, an individual's spiritual guide from the next world may purposefully not allow his counselee access certain types of information. That being said, in doing the research for this book, while many questions still remain open, it seems that enough information has been brought to light to reach the objective of producing a picture of a path that has a semblance of order.

The kabalistic information presented herein lays out the foundations and core principles of mysticism and contains, often in cryptic form, deep cosmic secrets (*soad*). Given the subject matter, it is not surprising that the writings are veiled secrets; hence I do not wish to arrogantly claim that what I have presented here is the final word. While I did consult with a number of respected rabbinical authorities on kabala, I was still faced with the task of combining the various pieces of the Zoharic puzzle with the empirical findings of the subjects regressed under hypnosis.

I was also faced by a dilemma. Newton's patients painted such a positive picture that I was hoping to be able to do the same by merely placing an additional layer from the Jewish point of view. However, this was not to be the case. According to kabalistic beliefs, there are definitely missing elements from the "positive-only" accounts of Newton's patients. So yes, there are passages regarding this journey that will undoubtedly be unsettling to some. Having said that, I believe the overall feeling garnered from exposure to this material will be quite positive and comforting, somewhat exciting, and certainly could have a lasting healing effect.

And for those who may wonder whether it is permissible to delve into the deep and highly guarded study of the world of souls, Rabbi Yuda'i bar Simon (Zohar Chadash, Folio 109) said: "Fortunate is he who tries to gain knowledge regarding the world of souls. For those who are successful in obtaining such knowledge, there would be no limit to his wisdom because he knows where he is ultimately destined to be in the future. As a result, he will make a concerted effort to be cautious in his actions in this world—and this is the essence of wisdom."

CHAPTER TWO

What Constitutes a Soul?

"Life is a great surprise.
I do not see why death should not be an even greater one."
—*Vladimir Nabokov*

THE HUMAN SOUL is typically understood to be the spiritual essence of a person, the entity that transcends our physical shells and outlasts our ephemeral life span. But the soul is actually far more complex than this. Its destiny is carefully chosen and planned out in the afterworld in preparation for its journey in this world. In this chapter we explore the various parts of the soul, touch on what roles these parts play, begin to follow where they are destined to travel and immerse ourselves into the rules of male-female soul compatibility. But before examining what inner components comprise a soul, let us spend a few moments circling the soul from the outside.

By conducting past life regressions on his patients, Newton discovered new details about the human soul and its journey, sometimes from one incarnation to the next. According to his patients' accounts, souls receive a road map of sorts before descending to this world, and although we may forget the exact details of this road map when we arrive here, certain markers remain with us. These markers are intended to help us recognize our life path and guide us in the right direction. How do we recognize these markers? After all, every day things occur that we could interpret as signs—what distinguishes the ones that are of essence from the ones that are merely coincidental?

A clue can be found in the Hebrew word "b'seder." B'seder is a common response when one is asked, "How are you doing?" Its loose translation means "okay." However, its literal translation is "in its proper order." The Passover feast, for example, is part of a "seder"—an orderly service of rituals performed by all those present, symbolizing key events commemorating the holiday. I have come to understand that when one asks how you are, by answering "b'seder" you are conveying your belief that everything that is happening to you is taking place in its proper order, or as it was meant to be. It is recognition that the path your soul is following parallels its predetermined life cycle. We struggle to recognize our souls' unique missions in our day-to-day lives, but in actuality, the divine powers inserted into a soul as it enters the fetus are strong enough to take control over the physical body, thereby necessitating that it will likely follow its pre-ordained path and the "signs" it encounters on the way. However, Rabbi Moshe Chaim Luzzato (also known as the Ramchal), a prominent eighteenth-century Italian Jewish rabbi, kabalist and philosopher, teaches that since we are born into an imperfect world, God limits the soul's influence, especially at the outset of our lives, in order to allow for the process of purification to take place via the performance of good deeds and acts of kindness through free will (*Daat Tevunot*, p. 58).

Man is generally not aware of the many adjustments God makes to his soul "behind the scenes." When the angel of pregnancy appears before God with a droplet of the fertilized egg, the angel asks what will be of this droplet—will it be strong or weak, bright or silly, rich or poor? If it will be reincarnated, then its judgment will be based on its actions in a previous lifetime. Nonetheless, God will step in like a father to a son or daughter and do things for the benefit of the soul without it asking and without fanfare. There are many "unclothed" spirits (exposed souls; those who have not aggregated the protection of Torah and *mitzvot*) wandering aimlessly who have not succeeded in connecting to their soul. The mercy that God graces us with often changes whole circumstances, so while a soul pretty much has free will, God does pull some strings in the background in order to give souls who are at a disadvantage their best shot at succeeding (Zohar Mishpatim, Folio 99).

In the mother's womb an unborn child must develop the physical attributes it will need to function in the physical world. Similarly, on Earth the soul must develop the spiritual attributes it will need to function in the spiritual world. This is the primary purpose for each individual's sojourn in the physical universe. Half the fun of "getting there" is in the challenge both the soul and body face along the way and the satisfaction garnered when successful (in finding love, in defeating the evil inclination or in reinforcing a positive trait). Sometimes we recognize the markers we encounter in our lives because the soul has some power over the body and it inherently recognizes these signs. But sometimes we don't recognize the signs because the body has some autonomy. In these cases in which the body is not in touch with the soul, ask yourself what your soul is struggling with, what are its strengths and what is truly unique about it. The signs will then become clearer. These questions are designed to open the door to understanding your unique destiny.

The Soul's Destiny

The good news in all this is that we are essentially born with all we need to know to live out our destinies. It's simply a matter of being in touch with our natural born instincts, gifted to us by God. The Zohar (Lech Lecha, Folio 78) recognizes this essential truth, and urges us to distance ourselves from researching all of the various philosophies of other religions in search of purpose. It is less important to understand the exact time and day we were born because our destiny lies in the hands of God and not in the formation of the constellations. Hence, we should turn inward and become more knowledgeable about ourselves, learn who we are and research the roots of our souls in order to be in the position to make adjustments and return our souls to the afterworld.

Though we may not see it, our soul knows what its goal in life is. The problem is the body. Our physical needs can mask the true objective our soul intends to achieve in this world, causing confusion. The body's desires and material wants can create a feeling of being anesthetized. Rabbi Yuval HaCohen Asharov, a widely respected Israeli kabalist, explains that the inherent light that emanates from our soul is darkened by the actions of our body, in effect clogging up the true light and true purpose for being. For example, anger is the most offensive quality one can harbor. When one gets angry, one's entire soul is adversely affected, so much so that the soul is actually forced to (temporarily) leave the body (Zohar Tezaveh, Folio 182b).

Notwithstanding the above, our bodies form a boundary that

separates one individual soul from another. We each have a distinctive space filled by our physical body and we work on distinguishing ourselves from others in how we conduct ourselves. On the other hand, our souls also unite us. Performing a *mitzvah* (good deed) for another increases the strength of the soul. Therefore, we must take care of our physical body, as it is a vessel for the soul to carry out these deeds. Rabbi Dr. Abraham Twerski, world-renowned author and psychiatrist, believes that it is not indulgent to care for the body by keeping it clean and healthy. If a regular regimen of physical exercise will help strengthen the vessel surrounding the soul, thereby allowing the soul to unite us and guide us, then maintaining a sound physical body is an obligation to which we must commit.

The Soul's Components

According to practitioners of the kabala, the human soul has three elements: *nefesh, ruach,* and *neshama.* The nefesh is the part of the soul that enters the human body at birth. It is the source of one's physical and psychological nature. One could say that it comprises a person's "raw materials." The next two portions of the soul are not included at birth, but can be developed over time; their development depends on the actions and beliefs of the individual. These higher developments are said to fully exist in people who are spiritually aware. An explanation of the soul parts can be broken down as follows:

- Nefesh: the lower part, or "animal" part of the soul. It is linked to instincts and bodily cravings. It presides over the propagation of beings and resides in the liver.

- Ruach: the middle soul, the "spirit." It contains the moral virtues and the ability to distinguish between good and evil. It causes the nefesh to act and determines its kind of action. It resides in the heart.
- Neshama: the higher soul, or "super-soul." This separates man from all other life forms. It is related to the intellect, and allows man to enjoy and benefit from the afterlife. It also allows one to have some awareness of the existence and presence of God. It is the supreme force issuing from the Tree of Life; *its* resting place is in the Garden of Eden. It resides in the brain.

The location of these parts of the soul corresponds to three major centers in the body. The liver, where the nefesh resides, is where new blood cells are generated. It is the will and desire of every living creature to grow and develop and preserve its life and life of its species.

The heart, home to the ruach, stimulates the blood to circulate to every part of the body. The heart also is a powerful expression of will. Through its union with the body a number of powers that are latent in the soul are set in motion, i.e., passion, appetite and desire.

Above the liver and the heart we have the brain, or the power of intellect and thought. It is with the mind that we must oversee and regulate our various desires. This is the level of the neshama.

The *Raaya Meheimna* (*The Faithful Shepherd*), a commentary on the Zohar, discusses two other parts of the human soul, the *chayyah* and *yechidah*. These parts were first mentioned in the Midrash Rabbah, aggadic literature on the Bible first printed in the sixteenth century. Gershom Scholem (1897–1982), a noted authority on Jewish mysticism who examined the origins and influence of the kabalist movement, writes that these parts of the soul "were considered to represent the sublimest levels of intuitive cognition and to be within the grasp of only a few chosen individuals." The chayyah and yechidah do not enter into the body like the other three elements of the soul mentioned above. Both rabbinic and kabbalistic opinions posit that there are a few additional, non-permanent states of the soul, such as these two, that people can develop on certain occasions. The chayyah is that part of the soul that allows one to have an awareness of the divine life force itself; the yechidah is the highest plane of the soul, in which one can achieve as full a union with God as is possible (Winkler, *Dybbuk*, p. 273).

Other examples of extra states of the soul include *Ruach Ha-Kodesh*, a "spirit of holiness" that makes prophecy possible and *Neshamah Yeteira*, the "supplemental soul" that a Jew can experience on Shabbat enabling an enhanced spiritual enjoyment of the day. This exists only when one is observing Shabbat; it can be lost and gained depending on one's observance. The *Neshamah Kedosha* is provided to Jews at the age of maturity (13 for boys, 12 for girls), and is related to the study and fulfillment of the Torah commandments. It exists only when one studies and follows Torah; it can be lost and gained depending on one's study and observance. Some people are judged worthy to possess a neshama, others a ruach, while yet others are simply given a nefesh. During our lifetimes we can develop the level to which we are able to acquire the extra elements of our soul (which usually takes an entire lifetime), and then climb to the next rung of spirituality. With additional *gilgulim*, or incarnations of our soul, we are given the opportunity to advance to the next level. A Jew who did not work toward perfecting (redeeming) his nefesh, ruach and neshama by virtue of learning Torah, even if he did mitzvot, would have to reincarnate with his nefesh, ruach and neshama together in order to learn Torah—it could take three incarnations until one completes the *tikkun* (literally, fixing or perfecting) of each of the three parts of the soul (Zohar Korach, Folio 178b).

Planes of Existence

There are three Godly worlds: *Atzilut, Briyah, Yetzirah*—these are the worlds in which God is hidden. In the world of Atzilut God is totally hidden, unreachable. In Briyah, God is reachable by the righteous. In the world of Yetzirah, where the angels reside, God does not always reveal Himself. Corresponding to these worlds are the three worlds of man: *Asiyah*, where the nefesh and ruach are in contact with each other; lower Gan Eden, where the spirits reside; and upper Gan Eden, where the neshamot reside prior to birth. The soul of a Jew never dies and never ceases to exist—it continues to be present in other majestic worlds forever. Therefore, despite the common custom to outwardly mourn the deceased (by conducting a funeral, sitting *shiva*, saying *kaddish*), it is also somewhat appropriate to (inwardly) rejoice when one departs from this world, for the soul returns to its original roots. It is natural for those left behind in this world to suffer the loss of a beloved friend or relative because we are thinking of ourselves and looking for ways to cope with our personal void. However, if it is possible in the midst of our grieving to imagine what the departed soul is experiencing, then perhaps we could also allow ourselves to be comforted by the spiritual advancement of the departed soul. Admittedly, this is not an easy thing to do.

The Non-Jewish Soul

And this brings us to a popular question: Is there a difference be-
tween the path of a Jewish soul and the path of a non-Jewish soul?
There is some disagreement in mystical circles as to whether only
Jews have such layered souls or whether other spiritual people do,
too. Rabbi Chaim Richman, noted Torah scholar and International
Director of The Temple Institute, answers:

According to the Torah, Jews must strive for connection to God
in this world through study of His Torah and adherence to His laws,
both of which are intended to enable and empower the Jewish individual to effect rectification, to literally elevate this physical world
to godliness. At the same time, the non-Jew is instructed to live a
righteous life, based on "accepting the yoke of Heaven" as manifested through a commitment to uphold the basic universal laws
of mankind known as the "Noahide code." This is a strict code of
behavior. It should be noted that the mode of this "acceptance" is
not left up to personal interpretation, but rather, must be expressed
in the form of an oral declaration before a *beit din* (rabbinical court).
This declaration must be an affirmation of belief in YHVH (the Hebrew name for God), adherence to His commandments, and a belief
in the authority of the Mosaic revelation of Oral Tradition. Despite
the seeming gap between the obligation by Jews to perform 613
mitzvot versus the obligatory seven Noahide laws for non-Jews, it is
no easier for non-Jews to achieve reward in the coming world than it
is for Jews. In point of fact, in the days of the Holy Temple, when the
Sanhedrin, the highest body of wisdom, legislation and social justice
was functioning, the Noahide laws—in some instances—were ap-
plied with an even more stringent judicial code.

Richman goes on to say that Maimonides (*Mishne Torah—Mish-*

patim, Hilchot Melachim Chapter 8:11) refers to *"chasidei umot ha-olam,"* righteous gentiles who abide by the seven Noahide laws. This classification, says Maimonides, is a very specific and significant spiritual upgrade over those non-Jews who do not observe the Noahide laws. As mentioned above, one must declare before a *beit din* of Israel that they accept these mitzvot because *Hashem* commands them through the Torah of Moses. When this is done, ordinary *"Bnei Noach"* become *"righteous gentiles."* Those who indeed observe these laws are entitled to a place in the World to Come. It is therefore conceivable that the souls of righteous gentiles take a similar path as Jewish souls do after transitioning to the next world.

Moreover, there are other activities happening in Gan Eden that affect the sanctuary of souls. For example, when a non-Jew converts to Judaism, it is as if he is reborn. He then has the opportunity to add an additional component to his soul—from having only a nefesh to also having a neshama. How is this accomplished? Well, the neshama is clothed by its ruach and waits until its time to descend to this world via Gan Eden. Every night at midnight God comes down to Gan Eden and is elated to be in the presence of the *tzaddikim*, the righteous, whose souls reunite with their soulmate wives at night. As a result of this union, additional *neshamot* are thus created and are held in the sanctuary of souls until such time as one converts to Judaism, at which point one receives his own neshama (Zohar Mishpatim, Folio 99b).

Sanctuary of Souls: The Beginning
of the Soul's Descent to This World

Interestingly, before the soul's descent to this world, its three components come together in a place called *olam haneshamot*, the "sanctuary of souls," located in a realm of upper Gan Eden called the *otzar* (also referred to as the divine treasury of souls, or *tsror hachayyim*, the bundle of life). This *otzar* is a transcendent realm of human souls in the highest spheres of creation. Before souls are born, they are said to come from a section of this treasury called *'guf'*, from which they descend to the earthly realm to animate human bodies (The Talmud, Avodah Zarah 5a, Nedarim 13b, Yevamot 62a) and they return at some point after death (The Talmud, Tractate Shabbat 152a; Pesikta Rabbati 2:3).

Imagine sitting or mulling around in a waiting room, a place where one usually rests until called upon to advance into another area or space. Such is the plight of souls, especially first-time souls about to descend to this world. So God provides a comfortable designated area in which souls can prepare themselves before their journey continues to this world.

According to the Zohar, after death each part of the soul undergoes a different experience. The two lower levels of the soul are purified and purged of physical and emotional attachments, while the higher level experiences transcendental bliss. These three levels separate after death, each returning to the place from which it originated—the nefesh and ruach each emanating from (lower) Gan Eden and the neshama from the Tree of Life in the center of Gan Eden (a full explanation of the different parts of Gan Eden is provided in Chapter 4). Immediately after physical death, the nefesh remains with the body in the grave up to a period of one year whereupon the flesh of the body rots away. As long as the flesh is on the body, the nefesh remains in the grave. As we shall see later on, it is during this time that (together) the body and soul continue to be judged for sins committed while in this world. Then after 12 months, when the flesh has completely disintegrated, the nefesh rises to lower Gan Eden and only minor sparks of it remain in the body's bones—there they become purified in the dust until they join the spiritual body after the ultimate Resurrection (at the End of Days, when it is said the dead will rise from their graves) (Zohar Shlach, Folio 170). The ruach also ascends to lower Gan Eden, where the angel Michael offers it as a sacrifice to the Almighty; and the neshama, because it is not subject to be tainted by sin, ascends higher to the Tree of Life (Waite, p. 244) and then on to upper Gan Eden. The neshama, however, cannot reach upper Gan Eden immediately because it is already accustomed to the base atmosphere of this world, and is not yet ready to blossom in a strange environment. It is likened to a chick that breaks out of its shell for the first time—it moves very slowly until it gets used to its new environs. Thus the neshama builds up new strength day after day so that by the end of the twelfth month it can literally soar to upper Gan Eden (Armoni, *K'Gan Raveh* p. 46).

Rabbi Simcha Paull Raphael, author of *Jewish Views of the Afterlife* adds that the chayyah and yechidah return to upper Gan Eden immediately after death and become unified with God. Those who have awakened these dimensions of their being are able to perceive the infinite grandeur of the divine realms, thereby meriting entrance to the ever flowing celestial stream—described by the Zohar as the "bundle of life." We shall become more familiar with this later on in our discussion of step #45—upper Gan Eden.

Soul Roots & Klipot

According to Jewish belief, Adam's soul is the root of all souls. Abel reincarnated into Seth and then into Enosh and then into other righteous people and finally into Moses, stretching over a period of 26 generations, until Israel received the Torah at Mt. Sinai. Our souls, comprised of our ancestors, current and future generations, are all descendents (or sparks) of the original 600,000 root souls who left Egypt. The Zohar tells us that there are 600,000 souls who stand and enlighten in every generation (Tikunei HaZohar, Folio 100). These are Abel's soul sparks incarnated from generation to generation. After Adam sinned, his soul was split up into innumerable pieces and fell to the bottom-most depths of the *klipot*, corrupted shells formed by the evil inclination that entrap sparks; it is the source of all that is wrong and evil. Klipot are also manifested in man as mistaken ideas, misguided feelings and ill-conceived behavior. Pinchas (Phineas), grandson of Aaron the high Priest, was formed from two of these soul sparks from Adam, one who had roots in Joseph and the other in Yitro (Jethro), Moses's father-in-law. We see from here that it is possible to have souls with roots from different soul sources (*Chesed L'Avraham*, p. 173). Interestingly, the Zohar (Tazria, Folio 43b) teaches that the soul splits into many sparks and with each incarnation a number of sparks goes along with it. The number of sparks is actually equivalent to the number of days that person is destined to live in this world.

During the course of a regular week we are all individually preoccupied in this world with efforts to pry away pieces of our own sparks caught within the klipot that engulf us. However, we are not always successful; sometimes sparks are so deeply embedded in klipot that they can literally put our lives in peril. Then an amazing phenomenon takes place. Every Friday afternoon toward evening (before Shabbat), the soul of Moses, together with a few thousand righteous souls from Gan Eden, come down to this world and try with great zeal to release all of those sparks stuck in the clutches of the klipot, thereby giving them a chance to rise and advance toward their perfection (Tikunei HaZohar, Folio 29b). What is also interesting to note is that from the time that the Temple was first destroyed, it is said that no new souls descended to this world, only old souls who reincarnated many times.

Forms of Souls

Kabalists affirm that the physical body and spiritual body are actually one and the same—before, during, and after life—albeit manifested on two different planes. In other words, the form that the body takes exists with the soul from its inception and remains eternally. After physical death, the soul is no longer manifested in the material realm of existence, but it remains operative on its original plane of existence, the spiritual realm (Winkler, *Dybbuk*, p. 269). All souls, prior to their descent into this world, are garbed in the very body and image in which they are destined to exist in this world (*Nishmat Chaim*, 1:13). This explains how we recognize friends and relatives in the afterworld.

After death, God personally paves the way for the neshama to free itself from the physical body and begin its ascent. How so? By neutralizing the *sitra achra*. The sitra achra, literally the "other side," is the name given to that "being" (forces of evil which underlie all of reality) created by God to oppose man and perhaps even to lead him to sin. It represents the extreme opposite of all that is pure and holy, and as such, is associated with spiritual impurity and death. It is responsible for trying to hold onto the neshama of a person at death, thus preventing it from ascending to higher spiritual planes. Consequently, during the transition from this world to the next, God literally takes away the power of the sitra achra and puts it to death, thereby immediately giving life to the neshama (Zohar Balak, Folio 205).

Recharging the Soul

At night, as we sleep, the soul is freed from the physical conditions of the body and the material plane of existence and often meets up with a discarnate soul (Winkler, *Dybbuk*, p. 75), the state or condition of a living creature that has died. Souls are thus recharged during sleep when they "get away" from the body for a few hours to get rejuvenated. "Most souls reacquire the balance of their energy at one of three primary spiritual stations after death—at the gateway (portal to the next world), during orientation, or after returning to their soul group" (Newton, *Destiny of Souls*, pp.119–120).

We shall come to discover that souls undergo an official orientation session welcoming them to the afterlife, where they are also assigned a peer group. Furthermore, every soul has a number of roots and each root has a number of sparks. When we sleep and our soul leaves the body, it utilizes the time to learn an aspect of its sparks, or true essence. The message it gets is directly proportional to its concomitant actions during the day (*Torat Hagilgul*, Introduction 17). This procedure of re-energizing cannot take place while in the body; otherwise, the body would literally explode from overexposure to the "light source," God (Rabbi Zamir Cohen, *The Israel Home Channel*, August 7, 2007).

Every night our soul rises to heaven in order to report to the *Beit Din* (High Court) on our deeds from earlier that day (Zohar Lech Lecha 92). On its journey between the physical world and the spiritual world, it must pass through four different kinds of klipot. If the soul did not become impure during that day, then these klipot cannot stop the soul from advancing upward (Zohar Lech Lecha, Folio 83). The soul then bears witness on every word said during the day by the body and holds these words before the High Court. Then they are written down on a note for future reference. Sometimes the soul will even ask the High Court to bring a punishment upon the body so that it might learn a lesson and have an opportunity to do a *tikkun* (Reisheet Chochma, *Shaar Kedusha*, Chap. 11:19). If the soul became impure during that day, then it gets stuck to one of the four klipot alluded to above and results in dreams construed of falsehood and lies. Thus at night we each get a taste of death via sleep, when the winds of impurity fly around and rest upon one's hands. Hence, upon awakening, when the soul returns to the body in the morning, one is commanded to wash his hands in order to wash away the impurity (Zohar Bereisheet, and Folio 53b). Just like Noah sent the dove as a faithful messenger, so too, a man's neshama sends its spirit as a messenger in order to become renewed.

More specifically, at midnight a voice awakens and announces that it is time to pay the righteous their due. All righteous souls stand in the shadow of their Creator clothed in new garments, bathe in the dew that is destined to be utilized by God in the Resurrection and gather round to learn Torah each in their respective yeshivas. After a study session, the souls come out and see Eliyahu (Elijah) the Prophet enter and exit the temple of the forefathers. The souls then stand in front of the forefathers, gathered in set formation by male-female partners, whereupon God reveals Himself in His light, unleashing great happiness. God then leaves Gan Eden, ushers in the horizons and strikes a big tree bringing forth a consoling wind. A voice then emanates from the branches of the trees and announces "in remembrance of the world's pact with its Creator and lasting for 1,000 generations." A standard of kindness from Avraham then arises and leads to a period of goodwill, happiness, healing, and rest for the sick (Zohar Omissions, Folio 303).

After these events God returns the soul to the body in the morning, even though it sinned during the course of the previous day. This shows that God renews His close relationship with each soul with a tremendous amount of faith (Zohar Chadash, Vol. I, Folio 23b).

In sum, we are encouraged by our rabbinic authorities to take an accounting of what we did during the day and ask for mercy, because night is a time that death rules. Just as man confesses before he is about to die, so too, he should do so before sleep each night (Zohar Korach, Folio 178). If one repents at the moment of death, then when the angel of death comes to slaughter, the angel Michael intervenes and prepares to take the soul himself to the next spiritual level. At the moment a person senses his end in this world is near, he should say *vidui* (confession) with conviction and concentrate on saying the first two verses of the *Shema yisrael* prayer. These two verses comprise God's Hebrew name in recognition of the ultimate sacrifice of a man's soul. Just as one's soul departs every night when the body sleeps, reviews all that he did that particular day and then submits his soul for the night to God, so too, we should say the *Shema* prayer and faithfully submit to the Almighty in the hours prior to death.

Those who die outside of Israel have their souls taken by the (destructive) angel of death. Those who die in the holy land of

Israel have their souls taken by Gavriel, the angel of mercy, who is in control throughout the land. Hence in Israel, one's departure from this world will be less traumatic (Zohar Terumah, Folio 151b). Souls in the exile do not illuminate in their divine clothing as befits their status because of the darkness of the exile (Zohar Chadash, Tikunim, Folio 114).

Soulmates

Another popular topic that fascinates the imagination is the concept of a soulmate. What is a soulmate? Do we always find our true soulmate? It's no wonder that people question this concept with average international divorce rates hovering around the 50 percent mark.

Every soul has a male and female part. Neither part feels complete without finding the other via the union of marriage. The Talmud (*Sotah* 2b) says that 40 days before one is born, an announcement is made declaring who is destined to be matched up with whom. This is the ideal situation—this declaration is focused on identifying one's true soulmate. It is our task in this world to seek out our true soulmate and join together in marital bliss. However, this task is not easy or straightforward.

Our texts (Tikunei HaZohar, Folio 100b; Shaar Hagilgulim, Intro 9) tell us that women have no need to reincarnate, as their tikkun can be done in heaven; it is the man who needs to do his tikkun in this world. Rabbi Chaim Vital, an accomplished sixteenth-century kabalist and writer, who is renowned primarily as the recorder and editor of the teachings of Rabbi Yitzchak Luria (recognized as the greatest kabalist of modern times), explains that because Jewish men are obligated in the learning of Torah and are subsequently rewarded through the performance of this central mitzvah, they become immune to the fires of gehinom (a form of purgatory or hell), thus rendering gehinom ineffective as a vehicle of purifying one's soul. Hence, they purify through reincarnation rather than gehinom. In actuality it is not altogether clear whether men have a pure choice to either reincarnate or enter gehinom because we do not know how much learning of Torah one has to do in order to make him immune to the fires of gehinom. The option of reincarnation has to be in place nonetheless for those who don't perform any of the mitzvot, because it serves as the training ground for him to do his tikkun. Gehinom would not help such an individual. Women, on the other hand, who have no concomitant obligation to perform the mitzvah of Torah study, can go directly to gehinom and purge themselves of any sins committed in this world. Therefore, the reincarnation route would be superfluous.

Notwithstanding Rabbi Vital's explanation, souls of women can nonetheless "volunteer" to return to this world in order to help their soulmate reach their goals (if necessary, she accompanies him through a number of incarnations). It is in this context that a man must be spiritually ready to meet his true soulmate. If he is not ready, he will not find her in this incarnation. It could be that he will need a lifetime or more to reach the level of spirituality necessary to even come close to meeting his true soulmate. So what happens in the meantime—does he not marry? And what of the woman—does she stay in the world of souls and only come down when her soulmate is ready to meet her?

The answer to these questions is complicated due to the nature of circumstances beyond one's control and our inability to predict our actions. Generally speaking, a man might well marry a woman who is not his true soulmate—this actually occurs quite often (Talmud, Tractate Sanhedrin 107). If a man prays fervently to get married, another woman may volunteer to help a man get to a certain level of spirituality so that he may then meet his true soulmate. It could also be that a spark from the soul of his true soulmate may enter the body of a woman who is not his true soulmate in order to enhance and quicken the process toward that true soulmate match. Thus, a man who is married to a woman who is not his true soulmate could have children and live an otherwise productive and happy life. It is almost as if he is "borrowing" another woman (and marrying within the confines of *halacha*) until he merits meeting his true soulmate. There are times when, due to a man's sin, he may have to wait many years before this actually happens. Meanwhile, his soulmate may be serving other purposes in this world until the time is ripe to meet him.

Soul Shuffling

Another aspect of this subject has to do with those who did marry their true soulmate, but due to some tragic circumstance, the soulmate died at an early age. What happens then? The Zohar explains that a man has to be very careful if he wants to marry a woman whose husband has died. She is then in the category of one who "has been taken hold of" by the Angel of Death—meaning that her husband was more meritorious than any of the following suitors, and hence the soul of the husband will not allow any subsequent men to benefit from such a union. The Zohar is explicit about the extent that the merits of a man can affect his chances of winning over a particular woman, even if he is not that woman's true soulmate. Rabbi Ariel Bar Tzadok, a teacher of kabala and pastoral counselor, explains it this way: If, for whatever reason, the person destined to be one's marriage partner fails to become so, God in His wisdom and mercy does a shuffling of souls. In other words, that aspect within the soul of another that makes that one our soulmate can be taken from the original person in whom it was placed (but who is now otherwise occupied), and given to another who is not occupied. In this way, our new partner, although originally not our destined soulmate, actually becomes our destined soulmate. Also, the one who was destined to be our soulmate now becomes the actual soulmate of the partner with whom he/she is with. This act of spiritual soul shuffling requires that God move some mighty mountains all for the sake of our happiness (Zohar Mishpatim, Folios 101, 102, 106, 109).

The Zohar continues this discussion regarding a woman who marries twice—what is the status of the first husband's spirit? The spirit of the first (deceased) husband brings up a case to the heavenly court against the spirit of the second husband in which he asks Hashem to put him to death. The woman feels this inside of her and cries. If the second husband is worthier and more meritorious, then God will send the spirit of the first husband to wander about for a while to appear in peoples' dreams. If he was righteous, he will bring good tidings in the dreams; if he was a scholar, secrets of the Torah will come through in the dreams; and if he was wicked, he will be the bearer of bad tidings.

The Zohar says that had the wife not remarried, her deceased husband's spirit could have derived pleasure and benefit from the performance of her mitzvot and grown with her (in a sense, vicariously through her) until she died, and then the two spirits would have risen together to Gan Eden.

What is, then, the purpose of remarrying? The answer is that the second husband may well be the widow's *true* soulmate. The question remains: How does one know if a widow is one's true soulmate or not, especially when there seems to be a risk associated with marrying a woman who was previously married? In truth, one cannot ever know for sure, so depending upon the spiritual level of the man at the time, combined with other calculations that only He can make, God may step in and provide him with another suitable mate, thereby foregoing marrying this particular widow.

Soul Complications

All souls descend to this world from *olam haneshamot*, the world of souls, in co-ed pairs. However, the pairs of souls get separated upon birth, as they are often conceived in different places and at different times. For example, it is possible that the female may be born before her male counterpart. In such a case, whereby the male is not ready to (re)unite with his soulmate, another male marries her. When her true soulmate does reach his readiness, what does God do? He sees to it that the other male (who married the true soulmate) dies before his time (assuming he is a sinner). The saying in the Talmud that "matchmaking is a difficult task for God, as tough as splitting the sea" (Sotah 2a) is not exaggerated: often it means that God will have to put someone to death in order to allow true soulmates to unite.

If the first husband is not a sinner, it is possible that he could still be put to death before his time, because it is possible to be judged without "a day in court." This means that there are times when God actually bypasses standard protocol and does not give an individual the opportunity to defend himself. For reasons that may not be understood by mortals, God will take the initiative and create a situation in which it would be possible for Him to soul shuffle.

Not allowing a person to have his day in court is an example of one of these scenarios that God employs when He deems it necessary.

This seems like a rather extreme solution. Why not just cause the couple to divorce? Rabbi Shimon answers: because God is doing an act of kindness to the other man by not allowing him to live to see his wife become the wife of her true soulmate. However, if the male soulmate is not worthy, then the first husband is not cast aside. An example of the above scenario involved King David. God took the soul of King Saul before David began his reign as king so that Saul would not have to suffer witnessing his underling reign over him and take the powers he once possessed.

Hence, when a man is about to take a woman for a wife, he should ask God to be merciful and introduce him to his true soulmate so that he will not have to be cast aside for another man (Zohar Vayelech, Folio 283b).

The various scenarios presented in this soulmate discussion are truly mindblowing. We are not accustomed to thinking (in this world) about our spouses as anything but our true other half. In the spirit world, however, souls are capable of telepathy—getting into the minds of their friends and feeling exactly what they feel. "They do this for reasons of empathy, a desire for understanding, and to evaluate the disruptive behavior of each other in the last life" (Newton, *Destiny of Souls*, p. 279). Furthermore, in the next world, souls help each other in the selection of the circumstances of their next incarnation (see section on Life Review, Chapter 4). For instance, those who make it an objective to get married and have children will have the potential to be saved from judgment in *gehinom* (Zohar Vayeshev, Folio 186b), as this would satisfy fulfilling the commandment to "be fruitful and multiply."

In the spirit of soul cooperation, then, it is quite possible that two souls pre-arrange certain (even unpleasant) roles they would each play in order to help bring one of the souls closer to learning his lesson and correcting a wrong he may have committed in a previous lifetime. Many accounts have been brought to light by Newton and others wherein souls play the role of an overly difficult parent or sibling. However, when they reunite in the next world, they remember the premise for taking on such extreme roles and therefore will have no spiteful feelings toward one another. It's like actors going on stage playing out the roles of bitter rivals, only to go out and celebrate the show over dinner afterward.

Let us also keep in mind that our souls each have unique paths to take. It is arguable whether a soul's fate has anything to do with the sins of its parents or of its spouse. What is clear is that before their descent to this world, souls choose to what extent are they willing to go in order to cleanse themselves of stains sustained in their previous lifetimes. They could accelerate the process by taking the "express train" or take a slower path on the "local." Have you ever given thought to which one you are on?

CHAPTER THREE

The Soul's Journey on Earth, and Beyond

"Every soul journeys down into this world with two suitcases. One is full of the challenges the soul has to face during its lifetime. The other is full of the talents and strengths necessary to withstand those challenges. The first suitcase is opened for you; the second you have to open yourself."

—Rabbi Aron Moss

KING DAVID SAID "For we are strangers before Thee, and sojourners, as all our fathers were: our days on the Earth are as a shadow, and there is no abiding" (Chronicles I, 29:15). King David understood centuries ago what rabbinic leaders have been saying for generations: Our time on Earth is limited, and we ought to make the most of it while we can with the tools we have been given. If the time we have been designated isn't sufficient to accomplish our life goals, then it is likely we will revisit the same or similar place with the aim toward completing the task at hand. In this chapter we shall delve into the near-death experience and point out how this path is different than the "real" transition into the next world. We will also discuss reincarnation and transmigration, but first let us do a quick reality check.

The idea that our real home is not in Brooklyn, Toronto, Paris or even in Jerusalem, is difficult to digest. After all, we relate our present experiences to what we know of our immediate surroundings and attribute our emotional and physical attachments to the knowledge gained there. Those of us who travel from one part of the world to another may experience natural wonders such as the Grand Canyon, Niagara Falls, Mount Fuji, the Great Barrier Reef and the Colossus of Rhodes. To many of us it may not be apparent that these miraculous places could also exist in duplicate form elsewhere in the universe. In my book *Understanding the After-life in This Life*, I discuss the arguments that insist life after death cannot be proven according to strict scientific standards. If indeed it cannot, are we being irrational in believing that we continue to exist after death?

Dr. Gary Doore, a scholar of contemporary philosophy and religion and the author of *What Survives*, believes not. Just as a scientist with considerable determination will, in the face of negative evidence or personal doubt, adhere to a favorite theory while testing it in the laboratory, so too, we can continue to believe in the possibility of an afterlife. In his book (p. 279), Doore summarizes:

> ...if believing makes us stronger, more courageous, more enduring for difficulties and setbacks, less prone to defeat and despair that would be the case if we adopted either agnosticism or materialism— then these are legitimate grounds for choosing to hold the belief as a working hypothesis... without such a preliminary trust, we wouldn't have the incentive and energy to undertake the spiritual discipline necessary to verify the soul's immortality in a personally convincing way.

With Doore's words as our foundation, let us now shift our focus to two well-traveled paths far beyond the friendly confines of our comfortable residences.

The Torah describes five stages related to one's departure from this world: death, transcendence, embalming, mourning, and burial. Transcendence, also known in biblical terms as "Gathered to the People," is when the soul leaves the body and continues on to another dimension. Within this stage, there are two major paths that a soul can traverse before it advances deeper into the afterlife: the near-death experience (NDE), or reincarnation/transmigration. Getting familiarized with both of these paths leaves little doubt that something awaits us beyond physical death, and will serve as a basis for further understanding what lies beyond those two paths.

Near-Death Experience (NDE)

The International Association for Near Death Studies defines an NDE as a profound psychological event that may occur to a person on the threshold of clinical death or in a situation of physical or emotional crisis. It occurs in about 5 percent of the population worldwide. Because it includes transcendental and mystical elements, an NDE is a powerful event of authentic consciousness. The NDE contains vivid images and strong emotions, usually of peace and love, though sometimes of terror, despair, or guilt. The near-death experience varies with each individual, but characteristics frequently include hearing oneself declared dead, feelings of peacefulness, the sense of leaving one's body, the sense of moving through a dark tunnel toward a bright light, a life review, the crossing of a border, meetings with other spiritual beings (often deceased friends and relatives) and a sense of overpowering knowledge and purpose.

Upon revival, the after-effects of an NDE or related experience are enduring—even life altering. They include feelings of greater spirituality and a decreased fear of death.

I have met many people who have shared their NDEs with me and most said that they were told by a deceased relative that it wasn't their time to die, because they either had a message to bring back to this world or had some unfinished business to complete. Their enthusiastic reactions to their newly found lives were strong and determined as illustrated by the following story:

On July 22, I was en route to Washington, DC for a business trip. It was all so very ordinary, until we landed in Denver for a plane change. As I collected my belongings from the overhead bin, an announcement was made for Mr. Lloyd Glenn to see the United customer service representative immediately. I thought nothing of it until I reached the door to leave the plane, and I heard a gentleman asking every male if he were Mr. Glenn. At this point I knew something was wrong and my heart sunk.

When I got off the plane a solemn-faced young man came toward me and said, "Mr. Glenn, there is an emergency at your home. I do not know what the emergency is, or who is involved, but I will take you to the phone so you can call the hospital." My heart was now pounding, but the will to be calm took over. Woodenly, I followed this stranger to the distant telephone, where I called the number he gave me for the Mission Hospital. My call was put through to the trauma center, where I learned that my three-year-old son had been trapped underneath the automatic garage door for several minutes, and that when my wife had found him he was dead. CPR had been performed by a doctor neighbor and the paramedics continued the treatment as Brian was transported to the hospital.

By the time of my call, Brian had revived and they believed he would live, but they did not know how much damage had been done to his brain or to his heart. They explained that the door had completely closed on his little sternum, right over his heart. He had been severely crushed. After speaking with the medical staff, my wife sounded worried but not hysterical, and I took comfort in her calmness.

The return flight seemed to last forever, but finally I arrived at the hospital six hours after the garage door had come down. When I walked into the intensive care unit, nothing could have prepared me to see my little son lying so still on a great big bed with tubes and monitors everywhere. He was on a respirator. I glanced at my wife who stood and tried to give me a reassuring smile. It all seemed like a terrible dream. I was filled in with the details and given a guarded prognosis. Brian was going to live, and the preliminary tests indicated that his heart was OK, two miracles in and of themselves. But only time would tell if his brain received any damage.

Throughout the seemingly endless hours, my wife was calm. She felt that Brian would eventually be all right. I hung on to her words and faith like a lifeline. All that night and the next day, Brian remained unconscious. It seemed like forever since I had left for my business trip the day before. Finally, at two o'clock that afternoon, our son regained consciousness and sat up uttering the most beautiful words I have ever heard spoken. He said, "Daddy, hold me," and he reached for me with his little arms.

By the next day he was pronounced as having no neurological or physical deficits, and the story of his miraculous survival spread throughout the hospital. You cannot imagine—we took Brian home, we felt a unique reverence for the life and love of God that comes to those who brush death so closely.

In the days that followed there was a special spirit about our home. Our two older children were much closer to their little brother. My wife and I were much closer to each other, and all of us were very close as a whole family. Life took on a less stressful pace. Perspective seemed to be more focused, and balance much easier to gain and maintain. We felt deeply blessed. Our gratitude was truly profound.

The story is not over!

Almost a month later to the day of the accident, Brian awoke from his afternoon nap and said, "Sit down Mommy. I have something to tell you." At this time in his life, Brian usually spoke in small phrases; so to say a large sentence surprised my wife. She sat down with him on his bed, and he began his sacred and remarkable story.

"Do you remember when I got stuck under the garage door? Well, it was so heavy and it hurt really bad. I called to you, but you couldn't hear me. I started to cry, but then it hurt too bad. And then the 'birdies' came."

"The birdies?" my wife asked puzzled.

"Yes," he replied. "The birdies made a whooshing sound and flew into the garage. They took care of me."

"They did?"

"Yes," he said. "One of the birdies came and got you. She came to tell you, "I got stuck under the door." A sweet, reverent feeling filled the room. The spirit was so strong, and yet lighter than air. My wife realized that a three-year-old had no concept of death and spirits, so he was referring to the beings who came to him from beyond as "birdies" because they were up in the air like birds that fly. "What did the birdies look like?" she asked.

Brian answered, "They were so beautiful. They were dressed in

43

white, all white. Some of them had green and white. But some of them had on just white."

"Did they say anything?"

"Yes," he answered. "They told me the baby would be all right."

"The baby?" my wife asked confused.

Brian answered: "The baby laying on the garage floor." He went on, "You came out and opened the garage door and ran to the baby. You told the baby to stay and not leave."

My wife nearly collapsed upon hearing this, for she had indeed gone and knelt beside Brian's body and, seeing his crushed chest, whispered, "Don't leave us Brian, please stay if you can." As she listened to Brian telling her the words she had spoken, she realized that the spirit had left his body and was looking down from above on this little, lifeless form. "Then what happened?" she asked.

"We went on a trip," he said, "far, far away." He grew agitated trying to say the things he didn't seem to have the words for. My wife tried to calm and comfort him, and let him know it would be okay. He struggled with wanting to tell something that obviously was very important to him, but finding the words was difficult.

"We flew so fast up in the air. They're so pretty, Mommy," he added.

"And there are lots and lots of birdies." My wife was stunned. Into her mind the sweet, comforting spirit enveloped her more soundly, but with an urgency she had never before known. Brian went on to tell her that the "birdies" had told him that he had to come back and tell everyone about the "birdies." He said they brought him back to the house, and that a big fire truck and an ambulance were there. A man was bringing the baby out on a white bed, and he tried to tell the man that the baby would be okay. The story went on for an hour.

He taught us that "birdies" were always with us, but we don't see them because we look with our eyes, and we don't hear them because we listen with our ears. But they are always there, you can only see them in here (he put his hand over his heart). They whisper the things to help us to do what is right because they love us so much. Brian continued, stating, "I have a plan, Mommy. You have a plan. Daddy has a plan. Everyone has a plan. We must all live our plan and keep our promises. The birdies help us to do that cause they love us so much."

In the weeks that followed, he often came to us and told all, or part of it, again and again. Always the story remained the same. The details were never changed or out of order. A few times he added further bits of information and clarified the message he had already delivered. It never ceased to amaze us how he could tell such detail and speak beyond his ability when he talked about his birdies.

Everywhere he went, he told strangers about the "birdies." Surprisingly, no one ever looked at him strangely when he did this. Rather, they always got a softened look on their face and smiled. Needless to say, we have not been the same ever since that day, and I pray we never will be.[1]

Dr. Melvin Morse, an Associate Professor of Pediatrics at the University of Washington, has studied NDEs in children and is the author of several outstanding books on the subject. In *Transformed by the Light*, he writes:

"After scientifically studying hundreds of these experiences I am convinced that the NDE itself subtly changes the electromagnetic forces that surround our bodies and each and every cell in it. This change is so profound that it affects such things as personality, anxiety response, ability to have psychic experiences, and even the ability in some to wear a watch. In short, people who have NDEs are 'rewired'...This energy is funneled through the right temporal lobe which is altered by the experience...and may act as antennae to interact with energy fields outside our bodies. This is one possible explanation for telepathy. . .the temporal lobe is a receiving system, one that allows us to. . .perceive the light that comes to us at the point of death."

Given the above, we must be very careful in our understanding of NDEs. There is a huge distinction to be made between the journeys that our soul takes when going through an NDE versus dying for "real." Major studies were conducted on the NDE phenomenon by clinicians and researchers such as Drs. Raymond Moody, Ian Stevenson and Michael Sabom. All agree that due to the temporary nature of the NDE, the soul only proceeds up to a designated point, after which it returns to this world.

Ninety percent of people who report having an NDE also report experiencing 12 out of the following 15 steps that were delineated by Moody in 1975:

1. The soul separates from the body/floats to the ceiling. There is a feeling of ineffability (an indescribable notion).
2. The soul hears the news/becomes aware of being dead/is overcome by a feeling of peace and quiet.
3. A buzzing, whistling, swirling, windy noise or music is heard.
4. The soul moves through (or is sucked into) a dark tunnel.
5. The soul has an out-of-body experience, the dissociative experience of observing itself from an external perspective.
6. The soul meets with deceased persons—could be friends or relatives (this includes relatives he has never met before).
7. The soul observes a celestial landscape and colors.
8. There is communication with a Being of light.

9   The soul undergoes a life review.

10 The soul comes up against the presence of a border or limit.

11 The soul resists coming back to this world.

12 After an initial period of silence (following one's return to the body), the person begins to tell others of this personal life-changing experience.

13 The person experiences positive emotions and effects on his own life.

14 There is a sharp decrease in one's fear of death and dying.

15 The person corroborates his/her experience with others who lived through the same.

This NDE journey is quite a different route than a full-on death. In the latter case, instead of returning to this world, the soul remains in the afterworld. As we shall learn, an announcement is made in the heavens 30 days before a Jewish soul departs from this world initiating a process that encompasses specific steps along the way. Most of these steps are not reached during an NDE.

Nonetheless, NDEs and our reactions to them have much to tell us about our culture's relationship to death. In *Transformed by the Light* Dr. Morse says: "We have ignored death and hidden it away in hospitals, where patients die in the cold company of medical machines. The fear of death has become all-pervasive and undermines our own happiness. NDEs are appealing in part because they redeem the ghoulish mess we have made of dying. To many, NDEs provide some of what religion has previously provided, a way to talk about death before it comes, and a glimpse of death as a passage rather than a termination. The NDE tells us that we all have an inner voice that, if only we would listen to it, would tell us that death is not to be feared, and that life is to be lived to the fullest."

I found myself primarily interested in learning how to use the visions that surround death to heal grief. I firmly believe that the more we treat ourselves to information gathered and revealed about the afterlife, the more we begin to gain a sense of comfort in knowing that it isn't "lights out" after we take our last breath. This discussion of NDEs is just the beginning of piecing together what we know about our souls' journey.

In fact, most of what Moody presents in the 15 aforementioned steps is not new to Jewish literature. In his book on the topic, Rabbi Chaim David HaLevi shows how each NDE step has already been recorded and has its roots in the Torah, Talmud and Zohar (Aseh Lecha Rav, Part II). For example, in the Zohar (Vayechi, Folio 250) it states that after death, the soul moves along from this world to the next via the Cave of the Patriarchs, which is the portal to lower Gan Eden (a certain plateau in heaven). Likewise, at death, man sees an image (a Being) that he has never seen in his lifetime. In the same section of the Zohar (Folio 218) it also discusses family members of the newly discarnate that come to greet him. (If the soul merits it, they come happily. If not, they appear sad and crying.) The Zohar (Naso, Folio 126) also tells us that all of a man's actions appear before God so that he (the soul) can give a detailed accounting. This all makes up the chronological life review process. Finally, in the Talmud (Bava Batra 10, Pesachim 50a) it says that souls consume a tremendous amount of information so that whatever was not understandable in this world will be easier to grasp in the next one. The parallels between these Jewish sources and the NDE steps are remarkably similar.

Both Newton and Moody each discuss many cases in which the two concepts of love and knowledge are reinforced and emphasized as the raison d'être of life—in this world and in the next one. The

Talmud echoes this belief and states that those who arrive in the next world with knowledge in hand are praiseworthy. Furthermore, those who lose sleep over their learning in this world will be rewarded with the saturating glow of the *shechina* (God's presence) in the next world.

Through these examples and others we see how parts of what a soul experiences after first departing from its body has a basis in Jewish literature. Only now in modern times are many of these beliefs being validated by the scientific community. NDErs descriptions of the life review, for example, insist that it is not like a judgment or punishment for wrongdoing or moral turpitude, but rather a highly instructional and enlightening experience, leading one to be motivated to correct misguided actions of the past. In reality, this is just the beginning of a process, and it is natural for one to feel some pangs of guilt or embarrassment when standing in the light of God. Many years before the scientific community even knew of the term "NDE," the Zohar (Noach 65b), in one of many places, alludes to the continuance of life by stating that when an accounting of our liabilities begins, we are accompanied by the warm light of The Creator—and hence the soul doesn't feel the full impact of its misguided actions immediately.

NDEs have taught us a great deal about what may await us in the afterlife; some of it awe inspiring, some beyond belief. But for the most part, what we learn both from Jewish texts and from the reports of those who have experienced near-death incidents, is that the afterlife is nothing to be feared.

Reincarnation/Transmigration

Some kabalists believe that the souls are reborn to continue their good work or to complete unfinished business. Not every soul manages to conclude its mission on Earth in a single lifetime. In such cases, it returns to Earth for a "second go." This is the concept of *gilgul neshamot*—commonly referred to as "reincarnation"—extensively discussed in kabalistic teachings. This is why, incidentally, we often find ourselves powerfully drawn to a particular mitzvah or cause and make it the focus of our lives, dedicating a seemingly disproportionate part of our time and energy to it. Our soul, in effect, is gravitating to the "missing pieces" of its divinely ordained purpose. For example, one may dedicate his life to the giving of charity or to honoring one's parents, opportunities which may have been absent in his previous lifetime.

There are 613 manners in which the soul connects to God, and those are the 613 mitzvot, *or deeds*, which all Jews are commanded to fulfill. A human body is comprised of 613 parts, as is the human soul, and each part corresponds to a mitzvah. The mitzvot need to be fulfilled in action, speech and thought. When during a lifetime a person fails to connect certain parts of his soul to God, those aspects of the soul return for another lifetime to complete the process. Rabbi Mordechai Zaetz, a lecturer at The Jewish Learning Institute, explains that it is possible that those areas in life that we are able to conquer without a struggle are areas that we mastered in a previous lifetime. Those things that are difficult for us may be areas that our soul is still trying to overcome. When God brings suffering to man, he is meant to accept it with love because God presents such challenges out of love. He is likened to a physician who loves his patient, but in the process of curing him, causes him pain by insisting he take a bitter-tasting medication (Zohar Bechukotai, Folio 114b).

In its attempt to reach perfection, a soul can undergo several incarnations. We will now examine this process, including the frequency and number of incarnations a soul can undergo, how "soul sparks" play a role, the transmigration of souls into inanimate objects, how souls learn from past lives mistakes, the notion of continuing from where the soul left off in its last lifetime, voluntary suffering and finally a delineation of the steps beyond reincarnation.

Reaching Perfection

Newly created neshamot have no choice but to come to this world. It is essentially decreed by God. All other neshamot, however, have a choice (free will) as to whether they will reincarnate or not. Rabbi Yehuda Srevnik, Headmaster of Yeshivat Nefesh David in Israel, states that this is true as long as the soul passed the requisite test of doing teshuva (repenting) through a process of purification (as more fully explained in Chapter 4). If the soul is satisfied with the spiritual level it achieved, it is left to its own devices. The choice not to reincarnate is not unlike passing a test with a low grade. If the soul would like to improve on its original mark, he is welcome to do so by reincarnating. There are times when the soul reaches this conclusion by itself, and other times when God takes the initiative and determines what will become of a soul. However, a soul ultimately always has a voice. It might beg God to reconsider His decision to send it down to this Earth, or even pray that God finds it an appropriate mate to marry, even if it's not necessarily "a soulmate." In such situations God has to move around pieces of His cosmic chessboard in order to make a series of events fall into place without overturning the applecart. And there are numerous ways in which the equilibrium of things can be upset. One way would be a situation in which God decrees that on its day of death a certain soul is to reincarnate immediately; however, should there be a delay in burial, the neshama would not be able to enter into a different body (Zohar Kedoshim, Folio 82b; Emor 88b).

A soul's free choice is also conditionally based on which of the three godly worlds the soul originates from (as was delineated in the previous chapter). For example, souls emanating from atzilut are limited in that they do not undergo punishment in gehinom.

Thus the gilgul of a soul continues until each of its components (the nefesh, ruach, and neshama) has been nurtured to perfection (Shaar Hagilgulim, Introduction 2). When a soul returns to this world for further development, only the unrepaired component is sent back—in effect, an independent spark of that soul. Other parts of the soul that achieved perfection stay in the next world. Generally speaking, only one component can be perfected at a time in a single lifetime (although Newton reports of patients who have said that it is possible to double up, admittedly placing a very heavy burden on the soul).

This discussion on the soul's journey toward perfection takes us naturally into the topic of yibum, the Levirate marriage mentioned in the Bible, in which a man marries his (widowed) sister-in-law if his brother dies childless.

If a righteous man dies childless, the child that is born through the act of yibum will be the reincarnated soul of the husband who died. Because the deceased left a spark of his spirit inside his wife when he lived (embedded within her forever), the subsequent children born to her through yibum will be considered as the deceased man's own children (Zohar Vayeshev, Folio 187b).

Furthermore, the act of yibum represents a full tikkun, or achievement of soul perfection. How?

In a normal gilgul, the nefesh, ruach and neshama (NR"N) do not reincarnate together. Only the nefesh reincarnates until it is rectified. Afterwards, in another gilgul, the nefesh and ruach return together until they are rectified. When that occurs, then the entire NR"N reincarnates together until the neshama is rectified, which completes the soul's gilgulim. Or, sometimes each of the three soul elements reincarnates individually (and achieves tikkun independent of the others): the ruach with another nefesh in another body, and the neshama with a different nefesh and ruach in a different body.

However, when a man reincarnates through his brother, the entire NR"N may do so together. Hence, the new neshama will not have to undergo an additional gilgul. It is said that the baby born (from the yibum union) will not die before his time because the essence of his mother's first husband's neshama remains in the hands of God and the child's soul is a spark of that soul (Zohar Chadash Vol. III, Folio 108b).

Nonetheless, regardless of yibum, it is possible to ask God for a long life in order to increase our chance of achieving tikkun for the NR"N all at once (as difficult a task as this may seem).

According to Rabbi Yehuda Srevnik, noted author and Torah scholar, whoever says the following verse every night is sure to have his life prolonged: "With my soul have I desired thee in the night; yea, with my spirit within me will I seek thee early..." (Isaiah 26:9).

Frequency of Incarnations

Between the years 1000 and 1500, Newton's clients report having lived an average of once in two centuries. After 1700, they lived once in a century, and after 1900, more than once in one century. Souls have the freedom to choose when, where and who they want to be in their physical lives. According to the Tikunei HaZohar, the lines in one's forehead can show whether and what number of incarnations a person has experienced (Tikunei HaZohar, Vol. III, Folio 126). Moreover, it is believed that a person's characteristics are based on lines on their foreheads, their face, and colors of their eyes (Zohar Chadash, Vol. II, Folio 50), which stay with him throughout his various incarnations. Some souls spend less time in the spirit world in order to accelerate development, while others are very reluctant to leave. The Guide, the spiritual being in the afterworld who acts as a personal counselor to a soul, gently implants the thought, "It's about time to consider returning to Earth, don't you think?" (Newton, *Journey of Souls*, p. 203). At this stage of consideration we don't remember our previous gilgul because, according to popular Israeli lecturer and author Rabbi Zamir Cohen, if we (intentionally or unintentionally) killed someone in a previous lifetime, we wouldn't be able to "turn the page" and live a new life with a rejuvenated and energized slate.

Soul Sparks

After physical death, we wear our "spiritual clothing" in Gan Eden. The more clothing we have, the higher the level of spirituality the soul has attained. In order to purify the clothing of the neshama (and of the body itself) and to rid them of the klipot, we were given mitzvot to fulfill here on Earth.

Before each incarnation, the neshama breaks up into a number of sparks which then accompany the soul to Earth (the exact number of sparks, interestingly, corresponds to the number of days allotted for its life). Each day one spark stands and (through means which are not altogether clear) warns man to fix whatever needs tikkun in that particular spark. One cannot wear his final spiritual coat until all sparks have been fixed. If that one spark was corrected on the very same day he was warned, then the spark joins the others who were also fixed. If he didn't fix it or sinned on top of it, then this spark stands alone outside of this group and waits until he repents, as it is written in Avot 4:13: "One who performs a mitzvah, buys himself an advocating angel. Likewise, each spark not fixed buys him one prosecuting angel who is not blocked by the mezuzah from entering his house. Consequently, he is judged in gehinom for those missed days of tikkun, and the neshama becomes embarrassed because it is naked from the clothing it otherwise could have worn (Zohar Vayechi, Folio 224).

The Arizal (Rabbi Yitzchak Luria) was known to give a sign to some of his students to indicate which souls were reincarnated from animals. He would say, "when you see brazen people and they have no shame from others, know for sure that in a past incarnation they were animals who could not make a sound, and just as they did not have any shame in the past, so too they have no shame vis-à-vis his fellow man" (Tikunei HaZohar, Introduction, Folio 13). We learn from this that man's nature doesn't change, even after death, unless he makes a concerted effort when he incarnates to correct character flaws.

With respect to unfinished business in this world, whatever one has not merited completing in this world, one will merit achieving in Gan Eden by virtue of fulfilling mitzvot in a spiritual sense. One may then wonder, why any soul would reincarnate at all? We have come to acknowledge that there are certain tikkunim that cannot be done in the next world (i.e. getting married and having children) and therefore require reincarnation. Likewise, there are tikkunim that were not successfully accomplished while in this world and are left to be "fixed" in the next world (Zohar Chadash, Bereisheet, Folio 23b). An example of the latter would be someone who had previously missed an opportunity to help a person in need while he himself was alive. Before having another chance to help, he (himself) died. It is possible for this soul to intercede on behalf of the same person in need through prayer and other means from his new vantage point in the afterworld.

Number of Possible Incarnations

During the course of writing this book I have been asked numerous times the following multi-part question:

If a soul has been reincarnated a number of times, thereby creating a number of personalities, which one will be revived in the afterlife? How many times can one reincarnate? Is there a difference between reincarnation and transmigration?

According to *Shaar Hagilgulim* (Luria's *Gates of Reincarnation*, Intro 5), most kabalists agree that the soul will be revived in the afterlife while maintaining its personality. Each spark of the primary soul has an entirely independent energy and personality, so in the afterlife the soul will be recognized as it presented itself in its various incarnations.[2]

We should be cognizant of the wide-ranging roles a soul spark can take upon itself in any one of its incarnations, and as a result we should be careful not to jump to conclusions about others. "When we see people who are victims of great adversity in life, this does not necessarily mean they were perpetrators of evil or wrongdoing of any kind in a former life. A soul with no such past associations might choose to suffer through a particular aspect of emotional pain to learn greater compassion and empathy for others by volunteering in advance for a life of travail" (Newton, *Destiny of Souls*, p. 104). "Karma may at times seem punitive, but there is justice and balance which we may not recognize in our sorrow" (ibid., p. 371).

Defining Transmigration

When one thinks of being reincarnated it is usually into the form of another human being. However, souls can be initially rejected from enjoying this higher status, and instead can be transmigrated in an inanimate object such as a rock, a vegetative object or in an animal, all which represent lower forms of existence. Kabalists explain that the Almighty fashioned His world in four ascending levels of creation: mineral, vegetable, animal, and articulate (the last translates literally as *speaking*). One way a soul transmigrated in a rock can elevate its status is if it comes into contact with a plant or blade of grass. The soul embedded within this rock would then have an opportunity to transmigrate to a higher plane, where a significant increase in opportunity for perfection exists. If a cow comes by and eats the blade of grass and subsequently a piece of meat from the cow is eaten by man, the soul gets closer to attaining its opportunity to advance. Ultimately it will qualify for the more conventional gilgul into a human being. There are also specific periods of time in which one can transmigrate.[3] Fortunately, for one who strives to follow the 613 precepts commanded by God, there is no transmigration—he immediately reincarnates into a *medaber* (articulate being) (Zohar Pt. III, fol. 178b).

Limitations on Reincarnation

As far as the number of times one can reincarnate, there are differing opinions. The Gra (Rabbi Elijah of Vilna, also known as the Vilna Gaon), an exceptional eighteenth-century talmudist, halachist, and kabalist agrees with most kabalists who say souls can reincarnate up to three times (for a total of four lives). If after the fourth life he is not purified due to apathy or lack of effort, then he will be considered a lost cause and will not be afforded another opportunity to reincarnate (Zohar Yitro, Folio 91b). Another source in the Kabala says that new souls get six incarnations if they are conceived on a weekday, and only one if conceived on Shabbat (Zohar Mishpatim, Folio 94). The neshama conceived during the week will likely be enslaved to the klipot of suffering, work, embarrassment, onus and craziness. A soul conceived on Shabbat will achieve tikkun during its (one) lifetime because it is influenced by Olam HaAtzilut and hence is not beholden to the klipot. If it does not reach its tikkun for some reason, it nevertheless will not incarnate but rather receive its due in gehinom.

According to the *Sefer HaBahir*, a mystical work attributed to a first-century rabbinic sage Nehunya ben ha-Kanah and first published in France in the twelfth century, a person can reincarnate again and again, even over the course of 1,000 generations. These numerous incarnations are a chesed, or kindness, that God does for individual souls in order to give them an opportunity to perform all 613 mitzvot. A classic example is a cohen (a descendant of the priestly tribe of Aaron, and forbidden to come in contact with the dead) who has never had the opportunity to perform the mitzvah of burying the dead. In a second incarnation as a non-cohen, he would be able to fulfill this mitzvah. There are also those who say that re-incarnating three times refers to the body of a human and additional incarnations are as an animal. Some opine that the limit on three incarnations refers to the number of times one can incarnate into a male. One further opinion is that if after three times the soul has not done its tikkun, it then incarnates into the body of a non-Jew.

Some kabalists argue that reincarnating is not preferable to remaining in gehinom. The rationale is that in gehinom the soul accomplishes its tikkun in a direct fashion. Reincarnating comes with a set of other risk factors that are not guaranteed. If a soul reincarnates in order to do a particular tikkun, it is possible that it will get caught up in another set of sins, and fail in its mission. Nonetheless, it is up to each soul to decide whether it is ready to face the challenges before it. The reason the soul of the wicked has a chance to reincarnate at all is so that the (wicked) sons of the righteous can be given an opportunity to be repaired in their righteous fathers' merit (Tikunei HaZohar, Folio 100).

The souls of sinners are subject to specific rules. The Zohar (Mishpatim, Folio 94) says we all reincarnate according to our level of inequities in the quest to be purified. We've learned that for the soul of the righteous, there is a risk in reincarnating due to the impending dangers and potential indiscretions that soul may face. However, God sees to it to protect the soul of the righteous and guide it toward a safe place in this world so that it can complete its mission without peril. If, for some extenuating circumstance, the soul still finds itself in danger or in a compromising situation, it will certainly not be subject to severe loss and punishment. It simply will incarnate once again (even 1,000 times) until it reaches its intended state of purification.

Another reason against risking another gilgul is the fact that it is more of an onus on the soul. One parable tells of a man who labored for 70 years and went up to the gates of Gan Eden only to be told that he did not satisfy the requirements for completing his mission. He is then sent back, but on his way, the *yetzer hara* (evil inclination) causes him to forget his mission and therefore miss out on his opportunity.

The Zohar does not state here why a soul might risk reincarnation. It is plausible to say that perhaps the soul prefers to be purified by the actual doing of a mitzvah in this world. Moreover, as we shall further learn, gehinom does not purify the souls of the righteous because these souls are immune to gehinom's fire. Hence, they must reincarnate. A third possible reason is that gehinom does not "treat" all kinds of sins—there are some that must be rectified in this world. How can we tell which ones can be dealt with in gehinom and which cannot? The Talmud (Yuma 86a) talks about four types of teshuva (repentance):

A If one transgresses a positive command (instructing one to perform a certain act), one can do teshuva immediately.

B If one transgresses a negative commandment (instructing one to refrain from a certain act), teshuva can be attained on Yom Kippur (the Jewish holiday of atonement).

C If one's sins are punishable by karet (the cutting of the soul from its people, causing premature death on the earthly plane and a severing of the soul's connection with G-d on the spiritual plane), or death by *beit din* (rabbinical court), teshuva can be attained only on Yom Kippur and through *yisurin* (suffering, affliction).

D If one desecrates the name of the Lord, teshuva can be attained only by death.

Hence, depending on the nature of the transgression, we see that repentance on Yom Kippur alone is not necessarily enough. The Baal Hatanya, Rabbi Shneur Zalman of Liadi, the father of Chabad Chassidism, adds in *Igeret Teshuva*, his work on the concept of repentance, that if one merits it, he will endure suffering in this world for the sake of his soul. The Chofetz Chaim, Yisrael Meir Kagan (1838 -1933), an influential Eastern European rabbi, halachist, posek (authorized to issue definitive ruling of Jewish law) and ethicist, explains that a little suffering in this world can often prevent a great deal more suffering in the next world (Talmud Yerushalmi, Chagiga 82a; Kohelet Rabba 7; Ruth Rabba, Parsha 6; Rav Yitzchak Blaza in Kochavei Ohr, p. 126). The Talmud (Chagiga 15) discusses the case of Elisha ben Avuya who suffered 150 years in gehinom in order to reach the good graces of *olam habba*.[4]

So even if the wicked were complete evildoers but had but a few merits tallied to their side of the ledger, when they die, God will reincarnate them to reward those few merits. God prefers to reward these wicked people in this world to prevent them from receiving any merits in olam habba (Tikunei HaZohar, Vol. III, Folio 11b).

Past Life Mistakes

Wouldn't knowing about your past life mistakes be valuable in avoiding the same pitfalls in this life?

As we mentioned earlier, if people remembered their past, most would likely focus too much on regrets rather than trying out new approaches to the same set of circumstances. In starting afresh, there is less preoccupation with trying to avenge the past. When an angel taps our upper lip at birth and we forget all the Torah we learned in utero, it is because God wants us to work at learning and thereby get credit for the mitzvah of making the effort.

We are given clues as to what our missions are in life; we get flashes from dreams, we are gifted with intuition, we are given benchmarks to help us remember our past mistakes and can even acquire extra hints by calling upon our Guide in time of crisis. Our eternal identity never leaves us, no matter what our current status or incarnation. Through reflection, meditation, or prayer, the memories of who we really are filter down to us in selective thoughts each day.

Even Newton saw the benefits of this: "In small, intuitive ways —through the cloud of amnesia—we are given clues for the justification of our being. Past experiences should not inhibit self-discovery in the present. However, the unconscious mind holds the key to spiritual memories of a general blueprint of each life" (Newton, *Journey of Souls*, p. 67). Newton also said: "Amnesia allows for free will and self-determination without the constraints of unconscious flashback memories" (*Destiny of Souls*, p. 372). If one is educated to believe that there is no life after death, he/she may fail to recognize the natural process that automatically takes place with death. There are those who describe this lack of knowing as an incredible injustice, for the passage to the next world is confusing and the spirit may wander indefinitely without the body, stuck between two worlds, feeling part of neither. This condition may persist until a spiritual guide is sent to rescue and re-educate the lost soul.

Picking Up From Where We Left Off

Have you ever imagined what it would be like to be reborn directly into an adult's body, skipping childhood and adolescence, and picking up from where you left off in a previous lifetime? Think of the potential time you could save.

Consider child prodigies. When Joey Chang was a 10-year-old in fifth grade, he was able to write any form of music from modern to classical in his head and immediately play it on the piano. Mozart was known to have the same talent. Similarly, those who have performed at least 610 mitzvot in a previous gilgul are given the opportunity to come back in order to complete the three remaining ones. In such a case, the piece of the neshama that comes back to this world may be well accomplished, having the benefit of 610 mitzvot under his belt. Or the neshama may belong to a mediocre person who just needs enough of an opportunity to complete the remaining three mitzvot. It would serve us well to recognize and respect the unique status each of us possesses in this world as we navigate our way toward self-improvement.

CHAPTER FOUR

Inside the Map:
A Detailed Tour

"Each stage of our existence is simply the step
before something greater."
Source unknown

G IVEN EVERYTHING WE'VE learned about the essence of a
soul and its journey, we can begin to further explore the
delineated path, or map, each soul follows on its journey
from this world to the next. When I started to put the pieces of this
"afterlife puzzle" together, I looked at the material from Newton's
regressed patients, studies on near-death experiences (NDEs), and at
the vast material present in kabalistic texts. Through this research,
it became clear that there were many parallels in these apparently
disconnected texts. An order existed surrounding the circumstances
of our transition from this world to the next. Other sporadic sources
discussed some aspects of "an order" to things, but in all the material I examined, I never found anything comprehensive.

It has long been my objective to logically combine the paths discussed by Newton's hypnotically regressed patients and the paths

outlined in the Zohar and other medieval texts into a sequential order that makes sense and remains faithful to each of these primary sources. After years of mapping the travels of the soul, 46 steps emerged. The journey begins 30 days prior to the soul's ultimate departure from this world and continues through its various stop-overs, until its final destination in the next world.

The steps proceed as follows:

1   Announcement 30 days before dying
2   Body parts begin to say good-bye
3   Each night the *tzelem* (Godly spirit) leaves
4   Pre-death or deathbed visions
5   Being greeted by the Angel of Death
6   Encountering the presence of the *Shechina* (The Almighty)
7   *Chibbut HaKever* (Judgment in the grave)
8   Experiencing *Kaf HaKelah* (The Catapult)
9   Examination by court scribe
10 Gilgul (Reincarnation)
11 Soul remains close to its body for three days
12 Seven days of mourning
13 Gateway to the Next World
14 Moving across through a light fog
15 Mosaics/Entering the Astral Plane
16 Exposure to Music
17 Entering the Holding Place
18 A reaching out to the soul
19 Remembering scent and taste
20 Meeting the soul's Guide
21 Homecoming
22 Orientation

Each step on the path to the afterlife is full of wonder and fascination. As we explore these 46 steps we will absorb the unique sounds, smells, and atmosphere of each before proceeding. Some of the locations on this path are so vast and full of activity that it may be a bit overwhelming at times. There is no need to rush through. Take your time as you reveal the mystique of each place. Close your eyes and imagine actually being there, if you dare. At varying stages of the trip we will be moving forward, backward, down, up, and sideways. The trip will be exhausting but ultimately rewarding. Be warned that you may be a changed person by the end of the trip.

Step 1: Before the Transition

Thirty days before transitioning to the afterlife, an announcement is made in heaven by the angel Gabriel of the impending arrival of a soul. God says: "Let the righteous men come from their resting places to go forth to meet him" (The Talmud, Ketubot 104a).[1]

At the moment of the announcement[2], verses representative of the awakening of judgment that only the individual's soul can hear are simultaneously announced in Gan Eden so that the righteous souls already there can prepare themselves to receive the new soul. At this critical moment when his soul is being called out, an additional spirit enters the body and clings to it (Reisheet Chochma, *Shaar Hayir'a*, Chapter 12:4-13; 4:6-7).

Incidentally, this additional ruach is what allows one to have the strength to endure the sight of the Shechina, or image of God, at the moment of transition (see Step 6). At this point, one can recognize deceased relatives and friends, looking exactly the way they did when alive in this world; there is an opinion that says our loved ones revert back to the age when they looked their best. If the incoming soul is righteous, his deceased relatives and friends are happy for him; if not, they are saddened.

Consciously, however, we are not aware when this announcement is made.

BACK TO THE AFTERLIFE

Step 2: Body Parts Bid Farewell to the Soul

While the exact timeline of our bodies' departure isn't clear, we do
know that the process begins here at Step 2 and continues through to
Step five (Reisheet Chochma, *Shaar Hayir'a*, Chapter 12:4-13; 4:6-7).
The Zohar teaches that there are five intermediary agents whose
purpose is to connect the soul to its body. They are remembered
by the acrostic spelling of the Hebrew words *"kol tzame"* (all who
thirst—for the learning of Torah), with each letter representing a
different agent. The agent types are **k**aylim (vessels), **l**evushim (garb,
attire), **tz**elamim (images, forms, semblance), **m**ochin (the mind),
and **o**rot (lights). Each of these corresponds to the five parts of the
soul: *nefesh* (vitality), *ruach* (emotion), *neshama* (thought/mind),
chayya (will), *yechida* (essence). One or more of these agents begin
to leave the body at this stage.

Step 3: Each Night the Tzelem Departs

The *tzelamim* (plural of *tzelem*, literally "godly" image) are one's
spiritual clothing (also referred to as *levush*), worn by the soul's
(spiritual) body. It is also described as the go-between between the
soul and the physical body (Zohar Terumah, Folio 150). When a
soul removes its spiritual clothing before it makes its descent to
this world, the clothing is hidden away for safekeeping at its home
base in lower Gan Eden, and its spiritual status changes according
to one's performance of good deeds and Torah learning in this world.
Thus the soul's clothing will be ready upon its return to lower Gan
Eden, whereupon he will shed his physical clothing (his body) and
don its spiritual clothing once again.

Our souls, if pure, outwardly transmit a very bright light. Our souls are composed of both internal *(pnimi)* and external spiritual lights *(makifim)*. The external lights are on a higher spiritual plane than their internal counterparts. They represent levels of higher perception that transcend our intellectual grasp. They hover above the (internal) conscious mind and illuminate it by radiating understanding. The Talmud (Brachot 5b) tells us that when Rabbi Yochanan exposed part of the skin of his forearm, he literally lit up a darkened room. This refers to the effect that learning has on one's soul—that it can literally illuminate a darkened room.

Thirty days before transitioning, all of these makifim depart, and at the actual time of transition they return in order to experience the suffering of death together with the body. The makifim of the neshama then go together with the neshama and ruach to their respective places in heaven, while the nefesh remains with its own *makifim* at the house of mourning (see Step 12). For each of the 30 nights before death, the soul leaves the body and goes up to see its place in the next world (Reisheet Chochma, Shaar Hayir'a Chapter 12:4-13; 4:6-7). The body is unaware that the soul does this because it is no longer in control of its soul. The *tzelem* (image) of man darkens in this world while the soul sits next to the Almighty (Zohar Vayechi, Folio 217b).

A variation of the above description comes from the Zohar (Terumah, Folio 142b):

On the eve of Hoshana Rabba (the seventh day of the Jewish holiday of Sukkot), when notes are revealed about a person's fate for that year[3], the nefashot of the tzaddikim travel around to see these tzelamim (images) of men. The officer in charge of the shadows is the one who removes the tzel from a person. He is accompanied by thousands of angels who take the tzel from each person who is slated to die that year, and raise it in order to prepare its proper resting place. Then the tzel returns to the body and stays there until 30 days before death.

Step 4: Deathbed Visions

Two to three days before transitioning, a person experiences futuristic visions.

In the Talmud (Ketubot 103b) we learn that on the last day of a tzaddik's life in this world, he is shown the goodness awaiting him in the next world. That's why it says that if he dies with "laughter," it is a good sign. God wants to tell us that dying is not the final station, and that although the process of death is perhaps the most sorrowful event in a person's life, He will make the separation of the soul from the body as painless as possible (Nishmat Chaim, Article II: 19).

There are many documented cases of people who have had deathbed visions; they get a glimpse of what and who awaits them on the other side. Often the vision will include close relatives or friends with a soothing welcoming message. I have found that this stage can be the most convincing to those who will soon be left behind that there is "life to come." It is especially powerful because the individual merits receiving this vision while still present in this world, and can then relay this message of comfort to those around him. The vision is not seen by the eyes or heard through the ears—it is the soul that sees and hears (Hagahot Zioni, Parshat Vayera in Nishmat Chaim, Article II: 21). The beneficiaries of this gift (those close relatives or friends who are in the presence of the soon-to-be-deceased when their visions were revealed) have told me that it literally changed their whole outlook on life because for perhaps the first time they received a direct signal telling them "there is an afterlife—things will be okay" (see Case 1 below).

At this time, man ought to do teshuva (repentance)—even if he cannot physically move (Zohar Vayikra, Folio 13b). A person who earnestly hastens to do teshuva on his deathbed, but could not complete this task before he died, is still given credit for his efforts. God links that man's intentions and thoughts so that it is as if he had performed the teshuva in its entirety (Zohar Terumah, Folio 150b). Thus his soul enters the next world in a purer state.

There is a wonderful story about Rabbi Shimon bar-Yochai, a famous rabbi who lived in Israel under Roman rule in 70 CE. He was one of the most eminent disciples of Rabbi Akiva, and is believed to have written the Zohar, the chief work of modern-day Jewish mysticism. According to legend, bar-Yochai asked God Himself to pronounce His judgment rather than leave it in the hands of the heavenly *beit din* (court). There were a number of people in the presence of Rabbi Shimon on his deathbed who witnessed him asking, "Who is there?" At that very moment, Rabbi Shimon seemed to disappear. Those in the room were speechless from the great fear that overcame them. While still sitting there, they sensed the smell of many different kinds of fragrances, and each felt their powers strengthening; then they saw Rabbi Shimon appear in his bed. He was talking to someone, but the others could not see who. After a short while, Rabbi Shimon asked his visitors, "Did you see anything?" at which point Rabbi Pinchas said, "No we didn't see anything, in fact we were bewildered by not seeing you at all in your bed for a while, and when we did see you again, the room was filled with fragrances from Gan Eden. We heard your voice speaking to someone but we could not see nor hear the person you were talking to." Rabbi Shimon then asked, "Did you not hear any other voice except for mine?" They answered "no." Rabbi Shimon then said, "Apparently you have not merited seeing that part of Our Creator which was just revealed to me. But I am perplexed that Rabbi Pinchas didn't see anything, because I just saw the exalted place reserved for him in *olam habba*. You should know that I was taken up and was shown all of the places reserved for the righteous, and I felt uncomfortable choosing my own place, so I asked to be escorted by Achia the Prophet, whereupon I chose my place and returned to this room accompanied by no less than 300 righteous souls and above them all Adam, who sat next to me and asked me not to reveal his sin to the whole world except for what the Torah mentions about it. But when I told him that my friends in this room already figured it out, Adam said that they should keep it to themselves because it would not be understood by others—not because the sin was so big, but to respect God's will."

At this point Rabbi Elazar, his son, approached Rabbi Shimon and asked him, "Father, what will be my status in heaven and where will be my ultimate place in Gan Eden?" His father answered: "Fortunate will you be, my son, in olam habba, but know that after your transition, many years will go by until you are buried beside me. However, in the upper world our places will be together, as I have chosen them. Fortunate are we to join those righteous who will be praising the Almighty while acting as His serving angels" (Zohar Omissions, Folio 309).

The following are a number of examples of deathbed visions told to me:

CASE 1

A week before he died, my ailing father told me that he saw approximately 100 angels of death who came to him and invited him to a party. He didn't want to go, because he knew they were going to make him sign the book of death. He refused the invitation. Two days before he died, he told his wife that he saw two bright stars advancing closer and closer to him. He felt calm and happy in their presence. My father died on Shabbat afternoon. The funeral was set for the next day in the afternoon. On Saturday night, I had a hard time falling asleep. In an attempt to sleep I closed my eyes and relaxed. The next moment I felt something in my right eye. I kept my eyes closed and saw a vision of my father who had his own eyes closed, but then opened them. My father looked right at me and then broke out in the widest smile I ever saw. The image then disappeared. Filled with much emotion, I felt that my father came to me to give me a message that all was well. This episode gave me a tremendous amount of strength and inspiration and helped me not only get through the funeral procession the next day, but also made me feel that this was the beginning of a healing process from the fresh wound I was now experiencing.

(Emil Entenberg, during shiva for his father Ludwick z"l, January 29, 2007, Haifa)

CASE 2

A man I knew that had a history of heart problems became weak and was on his deathbed. His son was with him in the room. Suddenly he said to his son: "My father is calling me. Can you hear him too? I have to go now—Dad is calling from a white light and beautiful

road. Call mother and tell her." Then he just "went."
(Marcia Lewison, by personal communication—February 13, 2007)

CASE 3

When my father was in the final stages of lung cancer in the hospital in Sarasota, I was with him for many hours every day. We had arranged for hospice care in the home, and he was to leave the hospital on a Tuesday morning.

The Wednesday before, when my mother and I arrived at the hospital, my father found an excuse to send my mother from the room. He then told me that he'd had a dream during the night in which he was a small child back in Mea Shearim (a neighborhood in Jerusalem). He could picture their "railroad apartment" perfectly. He could see all the furniture and other objects in his room. He told me that it was quite odd because he couldn't have described that apartment or remembered the objects in it before his illness.

I asked him how he had felt in the dream—if it was frightening—and how he felt about it once he was awake. He said that it wasn't at all frightening, but he was puzzled at its familiarity.

The following morning he once again found an excuse to send my mother from the room. He told me that he'd once again dreamed about his Mea Shearim apartment. But this time he was a bit older and he could hear voices in another room. He ventured out of his room in this dream and could see more of the small apartment.

I asked him again what he'd felt in the dream and then once he was awake. He again said that it wasn't at all frightening and he was still puzzled but now felt an eagerness to dream again to see what would come next.

Sure enough, the following morning we went through the same

ritual. This time he told me that he was an adult, still in the dream, and he walked toward the voices. In the living/dining room were all his family, including relatives he hadn't seen or thought of in half a century. He could see them perfectly in the dream and he felt very welcomed.

By this time I was pretty sure that my hunch from the day before was correct; that the dreams were a preparation process for my father's death. It seemed to me that being with all his relatives in this dream probably meant that his death was imminent...

When the phone rang I had no doubt that it would be news of my father's death...

(Alissa Herbst, by personal communication—August 3, 2007)

Step 5: The Angel of Death

When the Angel of Death arrives, he makes a distinction between the body and the spirit. In essence, he removes man's physical clothing. The spiritual clothing worn in Gan Eden is made from the compilation of mitzvot performed in this world.

There is a male and female counterpart to the Angel of Death. The male (Samael, also known as Notrikon) and the female (Lilith) are always together. Their power is at its fullest at night until midnight, after which it weakens until dawn and then dissipates altogether. This does not mean that it is impossible for someone to die during the morning hours. The Angel of Death does not sleep, and therefore God can summon him to do his job even when he is not at his full power. There are also situations, albeit rare, wherein a righteous person may bypass this step of the transition without receiving the "services" of the Angel of Death (Chanoch, great grandfather of Noah, and Elijah the Prophet are two examples). In most instances, however, many of us are unaware of the pitfalls of the klipot that surround us and hence are more vulnerable to succumbing to death before our time (Zohar Vayetze, Folio 160b). This is highly disconcerting, because we seemingly go about our day-to-day lives almost totally oblivious to the constant danger that lurks. With more awareness and initiative in avoiding compromising situations, we could be preserving more of the days designated for us in this world.

Right before transitioning, the Angel of Death appears at the person's feet[4] with a sharp sword in his hand containing three drops of a bitter serum (death starts at the feet and rises to the throat—The Vilna Gaon, Even Shlayma 10:10). The person lifts his eyes and sees the walls of his house ablaze, and in its midst the Angel of Death who is all eyes (a hint to the fact that he is watching over many judgments simultaneously). The heart is racing from fear, as the heart is the king of man's body, and the ruach then visits all the bodily organs and bids them farewell. At this time, all of the organs leave (begin to shut down). The organ and spirit then share remorse over their wrongdoings during this lifetime. The man feels like hiding (from shame), but cannot. He then opens his mouth, whereupon the angel throws a drop into it, and then when he sees he cannot overtake the angel, he submits his soul with eyes open (Zohar Naso, Folio 126b; Tractate Avoda Zara 20b). This is the hour when man is judged to sustain either an easy or harsh death. Furthermore, on the way to the cemetery, angels are proclaiming aloud the various sins that this person has done in his lifetime, thereby causing him much embarrassment (Zohar Naso, Folios 129-132).

We are all aware of heroic efforts doctors make to save the lives of individuals and the courage manifested by those who hold on to dear life—literally. How does one know when to fight for one's life in order to prolong it, and when it is time to give up? When one reaches this stage of transition, the soul of the righteous knows when it is his time to give his soul back to God. Physically, it is at a point beyond reasonable hope for survival—exactly what that point is medically is not always clear to physicians. If we see someone who dies "kicking and screaming," the soul could be well aware that it is his time to depart, but puts on a "show" for those witnessing this behavior in order to leave them with a specific message. Perhaps one of those present is struggling, and after seeing how the deceased fought tooth and nail up until the end, decides to incorporate this trait of resolve into his own life. Similarly, there are many lessons that we all take away from listening to eulogies.

There is a story brought in Tractate Bava Metziah about Rav Yochanan, who could not be taken by the Angel of Death because of his devotion to Torah learning. In exasperation, the Angel of Death dressed up as a poor person and appeared before Rav Yochanan with the intent to distract him. He asked the rabbi, "Why don't you have mercy on me?" At that point, Rav Yochanan gave up his soul.

Step 6: Encounter with the Shechina (Godly Presence)

The presence of the Shechina also abounds in our day-to-day lives. Before God judges us for a transgression, He sends us a present in the form of a mitzvah. We then have an opportunity to perform a chesed, or kindness, to mitigate the severity of the judgment (Zohar Vayera, Folio 104).

The soul then has an encounter with the Shechina. The Shechina is likened to a holy field of apples; its pleasant fragrance permeates

Gan Eden (Zohar Toldot, Folio 142b). The Shechina resides on the uppermost plane, referred to as Palace #7 (there are seven levels going up toward the Shechina.[5] This seventh ineffable level is a mystery to man and is referred to as the place where man's "eye hath not seen" (Waite, A.E., *The Holy Kabbalah*, p. 247).

The *Shechina*, accompanied by three angels, then appears at the head of the deceased. Of the three angels present, one does an accounting of all the minutes the person lived and how he spent his time. The second one lists his sins, and the third checks to see how much of the Torah taught to him in the womb remained with him. Upon confessing his sins, the soul then actually takes a leap for a very brief moment to the uppermost plane. His (spiritual) eyes are wide open and the soul bows down and praises the Almighty. The soul of the righteous leaves the body like a kiss (The Vilna Gaon, *Even Shlayma*, Chapter 10).

The soul proceeds to enter a cavern (the Cave of the Patriarchs) wherein there is a door leading to Gan Eden. This very brief step is designed to quickly show the soul his place in lower Gan Eden. There he encounters Adam, the Patriarchs and all the just, who give the soul a *pinkas* (notebook) as a sign for gaining a cursory entry to Gan Eden (Zohar Lech Lecha, Folio 81b). Upon seeing this pinkas, the *cruvim* (angelic beings who support the throne of God and magnify His holiness and power) open the door and all rejoice along with the soul. (Similarly, a pinkas is given to the soul upon arrival in lower Gan Eden in order to eventually gain permanent entry to upper Gan Eden if he merits it).

The reason the soul encounters Adam is to admit before him that he died due to his own sins and not due to Adam's (major) sin in Gan Eden. The three angels then escort him along with his Rav[6] or Guide, his father, other departed relatives and friends who lived in his generation, and is shown his place in Gan Eden (Zohar Vayechi, Folio 218, 218b). Three days before this, greeters work to decorate his room in lower Gan Eden. He also is shown wondrous lights (from the sefira Bina, a channel of Divine energy or life force) and 13 persimmon rivers, because the soul's spiritual reward is to derive pleasure from scents which are stronger than any other pleasure it can have. The Angels proclaim before the righteous "come into peace."[7] The totally righteous then proceed to their place and sit and take delight in upper Gan Eden. The soul then returns in order to grieve for his body during the seven days of shiva. If he is not on that level of righteousness, the soul is returned from Palace #7 to this world until the body is buried (Zohar Vayechi, Folio 218b), and then a number of angel assistants grab hold of the soul until the angel *Dumah*, chief of all the angels of destruction, comes along to take it to *gehinom, or purgatory.*

After the above interlude, the soul separates from the body. As Dr. Melvin Morse mentions in his book *Transformed by the Light,* based on a study done in 1988, the soul is very much aware of its surroundings. This is significant for those who grieve over the fact that they didn't have the opportunity to say goodbye to a loved one either because they were not present at the time of the transition, or the family member was pushed out of the hospital room by physicians or nurses as the moment of death occurs. Dr. Morse says that in fact the soul does notice a family member who intended to say goodbye but couldn't, due to circumstances beyond their control. When the soul leaves the body, he sees what goes on in the room and outside of the room as well. Hence, those who feel that they missed out on saying a proper goodbye could take some comfort in knowing that the departed soul was almost immediately aware of the good intentions directed toward him.

It is also customary to close the eyes of the deceased immediately upon the soul's encounter with the Shechina. One indication of knowing when this takes place is when the patient suddenly opens his eyes wide and it remains that way. After all, he just saw the Shechina. Closing the eyes enables the deceased to preserve the glorious image he just saw (Zohar Vayechi, Folio 226).

One way to ensure seeing this glorious image is by being careful in this world not to look at the light of the Shechina during the priestly blessing in synagogue, because when it comes time to leave this world, the person will be looked upon as if he blasphemed God's honor, and thus will not merit seeing the Shechina at the moment of transition into the next world (Zohar Va'etchanan, Folio 260b).

Step 7: Pain and Anguish of the Grave (Chibbut Hakever)

Judaism teaches to have faith in the Talmudic contention that death is simply a transition from one life into another. What the righteous person wants above all is to die fully conscious, to be in full possession of his mental faculties at the time that his soul leaves his body. It is a matter of absolute faith that the same One God who was worshipped in this world will be served in the World to Come as well.

For the less spiritually in tune, however, the process of extricating soul from body can be a bit more problematic. A soul that has become too fully identified with the body through sensual indulgence would find it difficult to separate. To accompany the body to its final resting place and to behold the putrefaction and the decay of the body is understandably painful for such souls. This state of being is known as *chibbut hakever*, the pain and anguish of the grave. At this stage each limb is judged according to the pleasure it had without the benefit of doing a mitzvah. The first three days after death, one's intestines are judged (this is the source for the stomach imploding in the *kever*). From day 4 until day 30, the eyes, hands and feet are judged together with the nefesh. The neshama goes up with the angel Tahariel to continue the purification process, while the body is left to rot in the ground (Zohar Vayakhel, Folio 199b). As it corrodes and disintegrates, there remains no body to receive punishment and hence judgment ceases upon its soul as well. Those whose time it is to depart do so, and those who are then deserving of peace and quiet get it. Those who are to be further cleansed will do so, each according to that which he deserves (Zohar Terumah, Folio 151).

Even the righteous are subject to the judgment of chibbut hakever. The angel in charge of the grave stands over each body on a daily basis and passes judgment, and does so at the grave as well. Hence, it is beneficial for one to be buried, where the flesh of the body will rot quickly (in the earth, as opposed to being in a coffin), thereby reducing the time one is judged. There are those, however, who merit skipping the pain of chibbut hakever (Zohar Terumah, Folio 151b). Ways to prevent chibbut hakever are covered later in this chapter.

In order to destroy the illusory identification of soul with body and avert the consequent pain in death, Hasidim would often engage in ascetic practices while still in this life. Particularly exalted souls would be able to achieve this level of consciousness through prayer and meditation, becoming oblivious to their physical body and surroundings. Upon approaching the grave, an announcement is made: "Whoa to the one who rebels against the King."

It is said that this stage is more difficult than the judgment at gehinom. The Zohar (Shlach, Folio 162) explains that here the ruach suffers along with the body because it is being deprived of its freedom to don its spiritual clothing. In an effort to mitigate this, there used to be a custom to do *hakafot* (seven processions) around the deceased before burial in order to chase away the undesirable spirits who could take control over the body (Nishmat Chaim, Article II: 26).

The Asking of and Remembering of One's Name

The earthbound disembodied soul can encounter a number of dangers. If it is unable to separate itself from the body even through pain, it can experience a decay of consciousness and turn into nothingness. Immediately after burial of the body, Dumah (Silence), the guardian angel of the dead wanting to prevent this decay, asks each soul for its name and asks the soul if he concerned himself with the learning of Torah and acts of kindness, and if he treated his fellow man with calm and dignity (Reisheet Chochma, Shaar HaYir'a, Chapter 12:44-47).

Rabbi Chaim Richman explains that the question "what is your name" does not refer to one's personal given surname, but rather is an allusion to tikkun hamidot, the recognition of whether we were successful in understanding what aspects of our character needed to undergo "repair" in this lifetime. In Introduction 23 of *Shaar Hagilgulim* ("The Gates of Reincarnation" by Rabbi Isaac Luria, in which he records the fundamentals of spiritual development and the journey of the soul), we learn that every man has a specific *klipa*, an impure force, whose origins date back to Adam. All of the world's souls were a part of Adam before he sinned. After he sinned, each of the souls was affected in different ways—some more deeply than others. For Adam's sin there is no direct repentance other than death. For the sins we commit in this life beyond those of the klipa embedded in us all, we are directly responsible and can make amends. The severity experienced in chibbut hakever will depend on how deeply each individual soul was mired in sin and what he did about it in this world.

This then brings us back to the issue of the name. Each person has, in effect, two names: one that is given by his parents, which has an element of kedusha or holiness (it is not chosen by mere chance), and the other, which is the name of the klipa, the personal name of one's evil inclination. Rabbi Richman emphasizes that the punishment of chibbut hakever comes as a result of not even bothering to make the effort while in this life to find out what it is. By making this effort one would have had a chance to do the proper tikkun and could have thus rid himself of the klipa instead of having it done for him by suffering at the chibbut hakever stage.

Some people suffer amnesia due to the shock of dying and are consequently unable to remember their identity. In order to dispel this amnesia, the learning of a mnemonic device while one is alive is recommended. For example, at the conclusion of every *Amidah* (the central prayer of daily service), the worshipper is instructed to "sign off" by reciting a biblical verse that begins with the first initial of his name and ends with the last letter of his name. This is tied in to an aspect of tikkun that is associated with that soul's purpose. Among Sephardic Jews, the child is initiated into his/her own verse at the bar/bat mitzvah. In this way, the worshipper reinforces the memory of his Jewish name at the end of every prayer service. Thus, in death, even if he is unable to remember his personal name, he will be able to remember the Torah verse (Rabbi Zalman Schacter Shalomi, essay on "Life in the hereafter: A Tour of What's to Come").

Hence, if the person recognizes his "name" and answers yes to the other two questions posed by the Angel as cited above, the Angel throws the drop into his mouth and the soul separates from his body with ease.[8] If the response, however, is "I cannot remember my name," then the soul will be freed from the body with difficulty as if thorns were being dragged over a piece of cotton. Four angels come and lower the floor of the grave. The soul is returned to the body as it was during his lifetime. He then endures the following (Chesed L'Avraham, 5:10):

A All of the seas of the world are brought together and he is thrown into the cold and bitter waters—as a measure-for-measure punishment for turning a "cold" shoulder to mitzvot.

B A sulphur river surrounds and enflames him.

C Angels of destruction break his body, and then put it back together, only to be beaten again.

D The light of the world darkens around him.

E Waters surround him.

F The taste of death engulfs him.

G An angel called "Suf" comes to bandage up head wounds sustained when he raised his head to do a sin.

H Sticks made of steel strike him.

I The walls of the kever hit him.

J He is thrown into a barrel filled with thorns where snakes and scorpions bite him.

The good news is that one can avoid all of this. One way, already mentioned, is by making the effort to research and learn the theme of one's own klipa. Beyond that, the following are additional ways to prevent oneself from being subjected to this step:

A If one is a *baal-tzedakah*, a giver of charity.

B If one accepts chastisement with love and without resistance.

C Doing acts of kindness on a consistent basis.

D Inviting guests into your home (not including relatives and friends).

E Praying with fervor.

Included on this prevention list is a situation in which one is buried on a Friday from five hours into the day and onward until the commencement of Shabbat.

In addition, kabalists say that whoever learns Torah can be added to this list. It is unclear how much Torah is to be learned and whether there is a minimum number from the list of five items above that need to be fulfilled in order to satisfy the requirement of avoiding chibbut hakever. Interestingly, though, a weighted point system was added by the Chesed L'Avraham (Rabbi Avraham Azulai, a seventeenth-century kabalist and commentator) to each of the following:

Charity – 2

Chastisement – 2

Acts of kindness – 2

Inviting of guests – 3

Prayer – 1

In his opinion, the total of 10 is meant to cancel out the 10 measures of harsh judgment listed above. The righteous do little time here because in their lifetimes they "beat themselves up" by limiting their material pleasures; the intense study of the Torah also tires out their bodies (Maavar Yabok, new edition, p. 218).

After all this, he is subjected to the judgment of worms, where the soul anguishes over its body. From there, he is taken to the Catapult (the next step) by yet another devastatingly frightening angel, who lifts the soul out from the grave (Minchat Yehuda, p. 135).

Another opinion of what takes place here is that five angels of destruction come: one to hit, a second to count the sins, a third to remove the light from the body, a fourth to bring bitter and sour grass from the mountains (retribution for having eaten from stolen goods) and a fifth to hit its mother and father (who already reside in the lower Gan Eden) for not guiding their children properly in the learning of Torah and good deeds (Reisheet Chochma, Shaar HaYir'a, Chapter 12:47). The latter is difficult to conceive. How can it be that the parents still suffer pain if they have already reached their place in lower Gan Eden? Shouldn't they be exclusively enjoying their peace and solitude at this point? HaRav Yehuda Srevnik explains that the lower Gan Eden (step 33) is like a hotel where a soul resides until it reaches olam habba, which comes after the Resurrection (step 46). Until that time arrives, the soul is still subject to judgment. He is responsible for *"pri maalalav"*—the fruits of his labor. Parents leave a legacy after departing from this world. If their offspring do evil, they too will feel the pain of their actions—even in Gan Eden. It is at this point that the parents can decide to undergo another gilgul (reincarnation) in order to do a tikkun (reparation) according to the circumstances of their offspring's actions.

Step 8: The Catapult (*Kaf Hakelah*)

In the movie *Toothless,* a 1997 children's fantasy film, there is the depiction of a place called "limboland"—a holding area for souls who are not progressing.[9] Does such a place really exist? Yes—it is called *Kaf Hakelah*. It is a place where souls find no rest; they are caught in a place where forward progress cannot be made (Nishmat Chaim 4:19).

At death, a righteous person merits seeing the *Shechina* and continues along his path toward Gan Eden, whereas with the wicked, the Shechina appears briefly and then departs immediately, leaving the soul in "limboland" (Zohar Parshat Metzora, 53).

In Samuel I 25:29 it says that the soul of the wicked will be ensconced in the Catapult. Hevel, an angel of evil who meanders through the world without peace, will roll the soul like a stone (Zohar Beshalach, Folio 59). This soul will wander from emptiness to emptiness in various and strange gilgulim over an undefined period of time until slowly its indiscretions will dissipate, allowing the soul to then enter gehinom for further purification.

One can be stranded in the transmigrated dregs of various worlds in the Catapult as a *domem* (rock), *tzomeach* (plant), *chai* (animal) or *medaber* (person) (*Shaar Hagilgulim*, Introduction 22). Rashi comments on the passage in the Talmud (Shabbat 51b) that souls in the Catapult are forbidden to go as they please. The soul desires to reconnect with its source, but is prevented from doing so, thus frustrating it to no end. The Zohar tells us (Terumah, Folio 142b) that the soul falls between the cracks of the klipot and turns into a being of destruction that has no peaceful rest. Yet it is possible through prayer for a man in this world to effect a change in the destiny of the deceased about to enter the Catapult (Minchat Yehudah, p. 194).

Besides the problem the soul has in maintaining its identity, it faces another challenge. All the sounds that a person has heard during his life continue to vibrate within his soul following his death, like clanging coins in a gourd. He is thus, unable to achieve the subtle stillness necessary to receive the angelic or heavenly voices. This comes as a result of "devarim biteilim," wasteful things done with no meaningful objective (Even Shlayma, 10:11). The nature of this "static" can be compared to the inner disturbances experienced by someone trying to meditate in silence.

In order to rid the soul of this "dust," it is shaken in the *Kaf Hakelah*. The sages say that two angels stand at each end of the world and toss the soul between them. It is almost as if the angels try to rid the soul of its accumulated psychic dust by putting it through a cosmic centrifuge until only pure soul remains.

Were this treatment not administered to the soul, it would be unable to silence all the sensory images and noise that it carried with it from this world and would have to wander in the world of *Tohu* (Confusion and Emptiness) for ages. In one Hasidic tale, a lost soul who has already roamed for hundreds of years in such a void cries out: "Would that I already had reached *Gehenna!*" (Schacter Shalomi, *Life in the hereafter: A Tour of What's to Come*).

The Courtyard of Death (*Chatzer Hamavet*)

The edge of the Catapult reaches all the way to the courtyard entrance to the Beit Din Elyon (upper rabbinical court). Two messengers come out from the courtyard and take the naked soul before the High Court in order to give an accounting of his wrongful deeds. The courtyard of the High Court is vast in length and width. There are three stories of rooms with three judges in each room. The lower story handles the harshest transgressions; the middle level the lighter transgressions, and the highest level the most lenient transgressions.

Angels of destruction then come, speak harshly and beat the soul with rods of fire. The blows are so intense that the soul disintegrates to the powder of coal. The soul is then revived. If the truth is not spoken before the High Court, more lashes are sustained. Another court records in a notebook how much time is left until the period of punishment has ended. The soul is then given the notebook to read. All of his sins are recorded therein. In order that one soul does not sustain embarrassment in front of another, each one has its separate space in good distance from one another. This is yet another example of the chesed, or kindness, God shows (Minchat Yehuda, pp. 137, 153-154).

Step 9: Examination by High Court Scribe

After the Catapult the soul comes in the presence of Safriel, a high court officer, who will carefully check the soul as if checking an *etrog* (a type of citron that according to Jewish Law is used in the mitzvah of the Four Species on the holiday of Sukkot and must not have any blemishes on its surface). He will then decree whether the soul will immediately reincarnate into a rock, plant, animal or person—or whether to proceed with the next steps that will lead to gehinom. Until the soul "signs off" on this stage of agreement, he will stay in limbo (Minchat Yehuda, p. 162).

For those who receive judgment in the Catapult, *gehinom* will come only after their reincarnation into one of the four objects/forms mentioned above.

Step 10: Gilgul (Reincarnation)

The quantity of mitzvot and Torah acquired in one's lifetime is what remains with a person after death. A soul's advancement depends on what spiritual level he arrived at when crossing over from this world.

In heaven one can gain only a deeper and richer understanding of his life on Earth. It is for this reason that souls, once they have absorbed all that heaven has to offer, apply for reincarnation, i.e., in order to attain further perfection. Reincarnation is also granted to allow the soul to right the wrongs it has committed.

Some souls are so filled with the light of knowledge and the warmth of compassion however, that the heavenly court, the "supernal familia," will engage in all kinds of tactics in order to reinvolve it in the work of saving and helping other souls still on the earthly plane. Reincarnation is an option at any point after the Catapult, Gehinom, the lower Gan Eden, or even after upper Gan Eden. The process repeats until a soul has built its spiritual body (Schacter Shalomi).

There is another approach brought forth (*Shaar Hagilgulim*, end of Introduction 4) in which a wicked person is granted three *gilgulim*—if he does not succeed in repenting during that time, he does not get an additional chance for another gilgul. Rather, he is sent to the Catapult. If he manages to graduate from there, he enters gehinom and will then not need to return to this world. God knows that by exposing the wicked to another gilgul, he may be enticed to transgress other laws and will come up on the short end of the stick versus his total merits. Therefore, in order to protect this individual and his merits, he does not allow another gilgul. On the other hand, a righteous person is often allowed another gilgul because he will likely add to his merits in an additional lifetime in this world, plus the endurance of suffering will further melt away his (few) sins, and hence enhance the total accounting of his merits.

Any of the three parts of a person's soul (the neshama, ruach or nefesh) can be involved in a gilgul. According to *Shaar Hagilgulim* (Introduction 8), the reasons for reincarnating are to: repent for sins, do a *mitzvah* not accomplished as yet, benefit others to guide them in their journey, and receive direction from another neshama. After reaching the nefesh level in one's lifetime, the next incarnation brings the ruach. It is possible to have a double gilgul, where two neshamot reside in one body (Shaar Hagilgulim, Introductions 4, 5). However, this is highly uncommon.

It is difficult to attain in one lifetime mastery of more than one aspect of the soul. Having said that, based on a verse in Job (33:29), Rabbi Chaim Vital (Shaar Hagilgulim, Introduction 5; *Sefer Hachezionot*, p. 352), mentions that it is possible for up to three reincarnated souls to reside in one body at any one time. Furthermore, it is possible for a soul to split itself up and enter two or more different bodies in order to accelerate its *tikkun*. This puts unnecessary pressure on the soul to accomplish much in such a short period of time, therefore it is not usually recommended by the Spiritual Guide.

Every righteous person has two souls—an internal one and a comprehensive one. The Zohar teaches that intent and thoughts of the parents during the time of conception can dictate how the newly created fetus will turn out. (While souls generally have free choice, and can select the circumstances in which they wish to be in their reincarnated life [see Step 36], there are still outside influences that can alter the intensity of the challenges they will ultimately face).

The soul of a person who causes another to sin, but did not himself sin, can attach itself as an "*ibbur*" within the reincarnated person until the tikkun is made (Schacter Shalomi). An ibbur is a transmigration of a soul into a body already endowed with a soul; in effect, it denotes possession. Ibbur has both positive and negative manifestations. Not only can the souls of the deceased be helped by those in this world, but the dead can return the favor. At moments of great danger they can come to forewarn their loved ones through dreams and visions, thereby helping them overcome various temptations.

A soul is said to have come into ibbur (literally, pregnancy) when it enters, in a benign fashion into the body and soul of a person living here on Earth (as opposed to a dybbuk, whose entrance is intrusive). Often such an ibbur can raise a person to great temporary heights.

Ibbur, however, can also help the discarnate soul who is in need of only one mitzvah in order to round out a particular incarnation. Instead of risking the danger of another incarnate existence it can receive the needed merit from the living by helping someone as an ibbur. The custom of naming children after the deceased is a means of affording the departed another return to life so that as an ibbur it can help the child and receive help in return. Hence, an ibbur can be self-serving or can serve the body in which it enters—in the latter case, the ibbur does not need to stick around to suffer with this body after it has accomplished its task.

An example of an ibbur in the Torah is as follows: When Pinchas, the grandson of Aaron, was living, the souls of Nadav and Avihu, his uncles, were reincarnated into him. Because both Nadav and Avihu did not have children of their own, they were not considered fit to serve as high priests. However, once they migrated into Pinchas he was able to inherit their greatness by becoming a high priest, and they received their tikkun by vicariously fulfilling the mitzvah of bearing children when Pinchas fathered his children (Zohar Pinchas, Folio 217).

While the case of ibbur is an instance of benign possession, tradition has recorded many accounts of evil possession, known as dybbuk (literally "sticking"). If a person was wronged by another and this wrong caused him suffering, whether in life or in death, the soul of the wronged can seek revenge by possessing someone (not necessarily the wrongdoer) as a dybbuk. A dybbuk can be educated in how to find spiritual guidance without harming the living or it can be appeased by offering the performance of mitzvot on its behalf. When it is recalcitrant, however, and refuses to leave the body of the possessed (although rare), coercive methods must be employed by a rabbinic expert (*Shaar Hagilg*ulim, Introduction 11).

It is possible for a soul who was in the body of a female to incarnate as a male in the next gilgul and vice versa. The piece of the soul that did its tikkun in this world will not come down in the next gilgul. Only those other parts of the soul that need perfection will return to this world.

The status of those souls who reincarnated is higher than those who haven't because they received their punishment and became purified. Those who have reincarnated have the possibility of reaching upper Gan Eden. Those who haven't can get as far as lower Gan Eden where there are spirits and souls from the lower worlds of asiyah and yetzira. Incarnated souls, on the other hand, have neshamot that came from the upper world of olam habriya (Zohar Chukat, Folio 182b). In one's first lifetime it is practically impossible to do a complete tikkun.

The specific day designated for incarnating souls, whether it happens at this step or after Steps 22, 33 or 43, is Friday afternoon right before the beginning of Shabbat (Zohar Terumah, Folio 136).

Step 11: The soul Remains Close to the Body for Three Days

For the first three days after the transition, the soul actually believes it will still return to its body. However, when the soul sees that the body's face has changed in the grave and the physical person is no more, it starts to distance itself from the body (Bereisheet Rabba, Chapter 100; Yerushalmi Tractate Moed Katan 83).

Step 12: The Seven Days of Mourning

During the seven days of mourning (shiva) the soul goes back and forth from the house of mourning to the grave in order to grieve for the body as it is written "...and his soul shall mourn for it" (Job 14:22; Zohar Vayechi, Folios 218, 226).

The reason we mourn seven days is to give the soul an opportunity to elevate itself. As explained in Step 3 above, according to The Arizal, Rabbi Isaac Luria, the nefesh part of the soul has two dimensions: the outer (makif) and inner (pnimi). Each of these dimensions has seven components. The inner part remains with the body in the grave, while the outer stays in the house of the deceased because it cannot bear to separate from the place of the deceased. However, the makifim also want to be with its pnimi. Therefore, after each day of mourning, one component of the outer leaves the house of mourning and clings to the inner part at the grave. At the end of shiva all of the seven components will have been elevated, and it will then be free to move on to the next stage in its journey (Chesed L'Avraham 5:31, p. 220).

It is at this stage that the soul is satisfied that the body has been well cared for, and can now allow itself to be free in its advancement.

Step 13: Gateway to the Next World

Now that the seven days of mourning are over, many newly transitioned people see a tunnel opening up next to them, right over their bodies, though others say they move high above the Earth before they enter the tunnel. At first it is very bright when still closer to Earth, and then in the tunnel it becomes darker and hollow, with a small circle of light at the end. There is a feeling of disorientation and of being tugged—the tunnel turns gray because the bright circle is expanding quickly. Then the soul is summoned forward out of the tunnel. It is unclear whether this step has any connection to the Cave of the Patriarchs (Step 32), the portal that leads to lower Gan Eden, or whether this is a separate tunnel that leads to a different set of preparation areas.

Step 14: Moving Across

The difference between functioning in the spirit world and on Earth can be summed up as follows: Movement in the afterlife is like going through soft translucent filaments of light. Earth is like plowing through thick, heavy moisture-laden fog or having concrete on your feet (Newton, *Destiny of Souls*, p. 351).

At this stage the soul moves across to the right, filtering through foamy clouds that are surrounded by a foggy brightness. This is a marked change from the feeling of moving upwards in the previous step.

Step 15: Mosaics/Entering the Astral Plane

Once out of the fog and on the astral plane (the spiritual counterpart to the physical world) the atmosphere is bright with sparkling crystal and glittery mosaics. The space is infinite, majestic and peaceful. Some may see wildflowers, castle towers, rainbows, familiar buildings or terrestrial mirages in order to bring comfort to the soul. Mark Macy, author of *Miracles in the Storm*, writes that this astral plane is reported to be much like Earth, perhaps even patterned after our world, for the primary purpose of making "new arrivals" feel at home. Researchers in many countries report similar memories of the astral planes (uncovered through hypnosis) describing concert halls, museums, hospitals, schools and homes much like those on Earth—but often much more magnificent. They are all set in landscapes of trees, flowers, mountains, meadows and rivers that are similar to Earth, but much more breathtaking. Newcomers can eat, though they no longer need to. Gradually such "earthly" pleasures are said to become less important. In any case, the astral planes are said to provide very pleasant and comforting surroundings for recuperation and spiritual growth after we die and before we move on to higher dimensions.

It is important to note here that souls and their current spiritual level are identified by their color:

Level I: Beginner (White, bright and homogeneous)
Level II: Lower Intermediate (Off-white, reddish shades turning into traces of yellow)
Level III: Intermediate (Yellow)
Level IV: Upper Intermediate (Dark yellow—a deep gold turning into traces of blue) Level V: Advanced (Light blue turning into traces of purple). Senior guide status.
Level VI: Highly advanced (Dark blue-purple surrounded by radiant light). Master guide.

(Newton, *Journey of Souls*, p. 103)

Interestingly, in one of his lectures entitled "Miracle World," HaRav Zamir Cohen of Hidabroot (an organization in Israel whose aim is to bring secular and religious Jews closer by providing information about Jewish heritage in a non-judgmental atmosphere), talks about the different auras surrounding an individual when he dons *tefillin* (phylacteries). In a study conducted at Ben Gurion University, 200 non-religious students volunteered to be scanned by an aura reader, from which the electromagnetic field surrounding each student was then converted by photography to a color. Students were to be scanned before and while donning *tefillin*. The "before" colors were almost all in the yellow category. However, once wearing the tefillin, the same students were surrounded by an aura of purple.

The results of the study showed how a person was elevated (at the very least spiritually) by putting on the tefillin. The tefillin, which is donned on the arm (near the heart where the ruach resides), and on the head (where the neshama resides) suddenly became a "tool of illumination." This was manifested by the change in aura from yellow to purple, and also via individual reported accounts of feeling more uplifted and sharply focused in their daily work and activities while wearing tefillin.

The faces of the righteous can take on the images of the sun, moon, horizon, stars, bolts of lightning, flowers, and candles of the Holy Temple. Each individual radiates his own image according to his spiritual stature similar to the color scheme described above. The commentator Ramban said that these faces will shine so brightly that it will be difficult to tell the difference between day and night in the next world (*Shaar Hagmul*, p. 445).

Angels are also reported to have specific colors. Michael, the minister of acts of kindness, is believed to exude a white aura, while Gavriel, representing gevura (strength), is in charge of notifying souls when it is time to depart from the physical body—exudes red, and Refael, minister of healing—green (Zohar Vayera, Folio 99).

There is also reference to colors having influence on a person.

For example, Jewish men wear four-cornered fringes (tzizit) that are partially dyed t'chelet (sky blue) in order to be constantly reminded of judgment, just as a soul enters gehinom clad in a cloth of t'chelet (described as more of a deep blue color (Zohar Terumah, Folios 139, 152b).

Colors also express the identity of the person on a spiritual level. It points to the make-up of a person's inherent character. The twelve tribes of the Jewish Nation were each identified by a distinct personal characteristic. Colors are also associated with water (white), fire (red), and wind (green) (Zohar Chadash Bereisheet, Folio 4b).

Step 16: Music

Music has been portrayed as a vehicle for connecting body to soul to God. The harp, lyre, trumpet, shofar and other musical instruments are just a few of the many instruments of musical accompaniment mentioned throughout the Bible. Psalms is replete with references to songs and music. The melodious tunes of the Levites during the period when the Temple stood and various angelic compositions are commonplace in the Scriptures.

Noise sensations such as buzzing or humming have been reported by those who survived NDE's. Newton mentions that people have told him they hear these same sounds when under general anesthesia. On occasion, resonating musical sounds with specific chords guide the incoming soul.

At this point in the soul's journey, Newton's patients reported an echo of relaxing musical vibrations, musical tingling, and wind chimes vibrating with the soul's movement like the resonance from the twang of a tuning fork. The soul feels a sense of healing, tranquility and revitalization all combined into one.

Step 17: Holding Place

The power of thought encompasses the soul as it is led to a holding place on the astral plane to rest—this can be short-term or the soul could take as long as it wants before continuing on its journey. Thus far the soul has been subject to many emotional tribulations. When one looks back to the path taken thus far, one could understand how a soul could be exhausted by now. This holding place, then, is a welcome pit stop for those in need of a "time out."

Step 18: Reaching Out

Thoughts of love, companionship, empathy and anticipation are waiting for the soul to arrive and are reaching out to it. Once the soul hears music, he also senses Beings of light humming in unison to welcome him back home.

Step 19: Scent and Taste

I remember being in the next world. I am not sure if it was in a dream or if I actually was there for a visit—in either case, I knew it was only temporary. The air was alive and fragrant with the scent of blossoms emanating from the cascade of flowers blooming in profusion all around me—bouquets of plush reds, vibrant purples, and brilliant blues—and I kept thinking that no one will believe that I was really here. So I thought that if I held on tightly enough to a flower, perhaps the petals would remain as evidence that I had really been to that place. I grabbed a flower hoping that I could bring this back with me. I awoke without the flower, but my hands were still clenched in a fist as if I was still holding it. The colors are still vivid in my mind (Sandy Erez, by personal communication, July 4, 2007)

A memory of scent and taste comes to the soul; it represents the more pleasant experiences from his most recent incarnation. There is no fear, but a feeling of relief to be in this beautiful place again. If the soul's life ended abruptly, he will enter the spirit world bewildered, sad, deprived and confused over leaving loved ones without warning. If he has further been traumatized by unfinished business, the first entity it sees is a form of energy—its Guide, a highly developed spiritual teacher.

Step 20: Meeting "the Guide"

In the early stages of transition, all souls encounter a wispy cloudiness around them that clears, enabling them to look off into a vast distance. This is the moment when the soul sees a form of energy coming toward it. This figure may be a loving member of the soul's family, but more often than not it is the soul's Guide.

The Guide welcomes the soul and explains that it passed through the experience called death, but that actually the soul is still alive, and maintains its conscious individuality. The soul is told that it now finds itself in the etheric plane (which is coexistent with the Earth plane) but in a different dimension, and that although it has shed its physical body, it has retained its etheric counterpart of identical appearance, but of another substance. The soul is also informed that its conscious spirit will always continue to live, passing through numerous planes of existence, with advancement depending upon its own efforts.

It is made clear to the new arrival that it will have constant assistance along the way, but that no one can force it to choose his path—the decision is entirely up to it. The soul is reminded that its energy is able to divide into parallel parts similar to a hologram and that it may live parallel lives in other bodies. Further, it is told that there will be a private orientation period with the Guide and that this is a time for counseling, with the opportunity to vent any frustrations it has about the life that just ended.

The soul is then told that its talents must be used, and that its innate capabilities for love, compassion, forgiveness, reasonableness, mercy, tenderness, unselfishness, sincerity, kindness, courage, patience, justice, and tolerance—must be increased to their highest degree in order to be able to proceed out of the etheric.

He who recognizes that this is something he must work on in this life on Earth, who recognizes his obligation to love his fellow man, will experience constant forward progress when his *neshama* reaches the etheric. And as his character improves, so do the surroundings in which he finds himself. There is great beauty, and it will be possible to hear and appreciate splendid music, spend time occupied by enjoyable tasks among friendly companions, such as a chavruta, or learning partner. The neshama that goes upward indeed lives in paradise. If the soul opts to do a certain tikkun, and return to Earth in order to accomplish it, it has the opportunity to choose its body—it can even try on different ones and experience them before making a final decision on which one to inhabit on Earth (Smith, *The Afterlife Codes*, p. 119).

The Guide, in a quiet meaningful encounter, will offer soothing words about the future of his family left behind. Younger souls move slowly through this phase—older souls move rapidly toward the gateway and often don't need to be greeted (Newton, *Journey of Souls*, p. 17) because of their familiarity with the paths and terrain from previous homecomings that followed a past lifetime. This same idea may have a connection on a religious level, whereby the Zohar (Vayishlach, Folio 175b) tells us that one who occupied himself with the learning of Torah in this world will become aware of special paths to follow in the next world, seemingly without the need of a Guide.

As spiritual teachers with a warm loving and creative power, Guides give souls awareness of the continuity of life. They are compassionate without being too easy on the soul. They are not judgmental or coercive—a soul does not have to do things suggested by its Guide. They build morale and instill confidence and courage. An example of this is having the Guide incarnate as his student's son (Newton, *Journey of Souls*, Case #18).

The Guide never takes on the role of a soulmate. Guides can be summoned via meditation *(hitbodidut)*, but cannot assist a soul in his progress until it is ready to make the necessary changes to take full advantage of life's opportunities. They want us to interpret our past lives so we will be able to analyze our mistakes. They are able to place a screen on their thoughts so that souls can't read their minds completely. Guides implant information and ideas, which the soul assumes are inspiration. The soul shouldn't experience grief too intensely because it will hinder its receptiveness, but Guides have to be careful not to make life too easy for a soul either.

In another context, the role of the Guide is to give a sense of order and clarity to the soul. We believe that our brain's main function is to remember. However, according to Rabbi Moshe Armoni in his book *K'Gan Raveh*, the main asset of our brain is its ability to forget! If a man thinks of his wedding day all the time, he will not be able to function productively because his mind will always be focused on the sheer happiness of the moment. Likewise, if he focuses on the death of his parents every day, he will also not function due to the overflow of grief. When one dies, all of the happenings of his just ended life in this world will flow into his memory, like the life review, and it becomes very difficult for the soul to think clearly. Thus the Guide takes on an especially important role in assisting the soul to "forget" that which he does not need to retain at the moment, and move on in a more relaxed state.

It appears to be a law of the universe that growth is always possible. According to many accounts, a Guide's mission is to counsel newcomers who want to learn and grow in the spirit world. Those who are lacking emotional growth, or who have lived unloving, resentful, vengeful, or selfish lives will be given the opportunity to serve and help others in order that they may advance to higher realms. They may even come back to Earth as spiritual helpers, like guardian angels, to influence people to avoid misdeeds and harmful lifestyles, and to overcome unloving attitudes. Those who have passed on often come back to their descendants to help and protect them. In so doing, spiritual growth takes place for both.

Step 21: Homecoming

A reception committee is planned in advance. The soul is greeted and embraced by entities who are not necessarily members of his peer (learning) group. The encounters experienced here are merely a prelude to the eventual placement within a specific group of souls who are at the same maturity level. A more formal reception takes place then (see Step 26).

The receptions at this stage are from entities that were close to the soul, but are on different developmental levels spiritually. The fact that they come to greet the soul now is more out of love and

BACK TO THE AFTERLIFE

kindness. They realize they may not have many opportunities to meet since the newly arrived soul will be busy with its own learning group. The level of celebration of the welcoming parties changes after each life. Older souls may not require a reception at all, as spiritual comfort becomes less necessary over time (Newton, ibid., pp. 34–35).

We have learned that souls have the ability to divide their essence. All souls who come to Earth leave a part of their energy behind in the spirit world. So if someone you loved died 30 years before you and has since reincarnated, you can see him again upon your arrival at this homecoming reception. The percentages of energy that souls leave behind vary—most take only 5-10 percent with them to Earth, otherwise it would blow the circuits of the brain. "Having all the soul's energy capacity in one body would negate the whole process of growth for the soul on Earth because it would have no challenge coping with the brain" (Newton, *Destiny of Souls*, p. 117).

Full awareness would have another adverse effect. We would experience a higher level of spiritual memory retention in each human body. "Amnesia forces us to go into the testing area of the laboratory of Earth without the answers for the tasks we were sent here to accomplish. Amnesia also relieves us of the baggage of past failures so we may use new approaches with more confidence" (Newton, *Destiny of Souls*, p. 116).

Step 22: Orientation

Certain souls who have done evil undergo separation in the spirit world. This occurs at the time of orientation with their Guides. Soul isolation (or seclusion) prevents them from mixing with other entities in the conventional manner for quite a while. According to

Newton, this is not punishment, but a kind of purgatory to restructure self-awareness. This "remodeling" also revolves around the law of karma (whatever you do to others will be done to you, in this or any future incarnation of your soul)—the soul undergoes intensive 1:1 with his Guide and often will incarnate right away in order to right the wrong he did (Newton, *Journey of Souls*, p. 49).

Suicides also fall into this category. These souls feel diminished in the eyes of their Guides and group peers because they broke a covenant. There is a loss of pride from a wasted opportunity. Life is a gift, and a great deal of thought has gone into allocating certain bodies for our use. The Guides think suicide is an act of gross immaturity and the abrogation of responsibility. Our spiritual masters have placed their trust in our courage to finish life with functional bodies in a normal fashion, no matter how difficult. If we do not show that courage, the same test grows more difficult with each new life that is terminated prematurely. These souls incarnate quickly again or, if not quite ready yet, go to a place of isolation where there is beautiful scenery but no other life forms with which to interact (Newton, *Destiny of Souls*, p. 153).

Step 23: Time of Counseling and Healing

Also known as the "shower of healing," this is a place of rehabilitation or convalescence for returning souls. The space is relatively small, clad with intimate conference areas designed to make the newly arrived soul comfortable, though his mental attitude can be quite defensive. Here the soul has a substantial counseling session with his Guide, whose goal is to debrief and bring comfort to the returning soul. When orientation is upsetting to a subject, it is because of the abruptness with which a soul is once again in full possession of all past knowledge. After physical death, the soul has a sudden influx of perception. For example, the stupid things we did in life hit us hard in orientation. This shower is intended for individual purification—to repair Earth damage, to remodel a soul who has absorbed too much negative energy from Earth. The shower is intended to help the more extreme cases.

In a dream that noted scholar Rabbi Natan Salem once had (as recorded in the book *Birkat Yosef*), he saw that the light of the shower purifies the soul and the Torah removes the stains sustained on Earth and cleanses and repairs the soul and returns it to its former unblemished state (Aseh Lecha Rav, p. 70). Rabbi Salem and his esteemed colleague Rabbi Yoseph Yedid were known to have made an agreement. They each swore that whoever died first would come back to the other in a dream and report on what it is like in the next world, and explain how God passes down judgment based on our actions in this world. Rabbi Yedid was first to arrive in the next world, and he indeed reported back to Rabbi Salem that all of the pages of the Talmud that he learned in his lifetime stood as a shield at the entrance gate to gehinom and had prevented his soul from entering, protecting him from any punishment. This corresponds to the discourse at the end of Tractate Chagiga (27a), where it says that the fire of *gehinom* cannot control *talmidei chachamim*—brilliant students of Torah. For those who learned Torah for its own sake (*lishma*), upon departing from this world, their souls will be defended as the Torah announces to all the angels of destruction it encounters along its path, not to dare come close. Likewise, the merits accumulated through the learning of Torah during one's lifetime watch over the body in the grave and walk in front of the soul when it rises to continue its journey.

Step 24: Transition/Weighing In

After orientation, souls move to a central port called the staging area. It is the area en route to their final destinations. One of Newton's clients described this area as "the hub of a great wagon wheel, where we are transported from a center along the spokes to our designated places" (Newton, *Journey of Souls*, p. 71).

The Zohar (Mishpatim, Folio 95b) describes an area that is large enough for two scales to be contained within. On one side of the area is a scale that is set within the realm of kedusha, or holiness, and on the other side of the area (separated by a pillar) is a scale set in the realm of the impure force, where the klipa called *Noga* awaits to extort and oppress the soul. These scales of justice never rest and are constantly in use. A soul "weighs in" on its merits to determine the level of spirituality it achieved in the last incarnation. Its destination is thus designated. Similarly, a corresponding "weigh in" is conducted before choosing a new body for the next descent (see Step 37).

Step 25: Cluster Group Placement

All souls are given a dwelling in olam habba according to their merit, as it is written: "...every man is given a room in accordance with his rank." (Talmud, Shabbat 152a). Hence, the soul's home base in the afterworld is set according to the spiritual level achieved at the close of his last lifetime.

However the soul is not alone at his home base—he dwells with other souls, mostly intimate old friends, whose spiritual level is about the same as his. Like Newton, Rabbi Chaim Vital specifically talks about soul groups in *Sefer Hachezionot.*[11] Rabbi Yehuda Ftaya, a leading nineteenth-century kabalist, also refers to souls connecting with others in the next world who are on the same level of spirituality. Souls who have the same awareness level are placed in their designated spaces with a cluster group (or home cluster), a small primary unit of entities who have direct and frequent contact with one another. Each group contains 3 to 25 souls, averaging 15.

From the staging area higher beings push souls toward their home base, as if going down a stream. On its way to "home base" the soul sees other clusters. It is possible to see familiar faces passing by. As the soul gets closer to his home base, he feels pleasure, sees masses of bright light, hears a cacophony of many voices and musical sounds, and is filled with conjured-up images of familiar surroundings from a previous life, such as a house or garden.

Many of Newton's study patients have reported that souls utilize humor in the next world in order to build camaraderie within the cluster group. When returning to this world, a piece of that sense of humor is within all of us. We just have to allow it to develop.

Step 26: Group Orientation

The soul's "peer" group then comes out to meet him. He is made to feel very welcome. Some dimmer lights also come to greet the soul. These are souls who split their energy in order to incarnate and therefore do not shine as brightly.[10]

Upon greeting a new soul, the group is arranged in a half circle and the new soul is welcomed into the middle. The Guide is positioned behind the soul at approximately 7 o'clock (back left). The first soul to come forward to greet him is always a soul of significance (i.e., a wife). One of Newton's patients described it as such: "She cups my face in her hands...she gives me a soft, gentle kiss and then hugs my head" (Newton, *Destiny of Souls*, p. 28).

There is no hatred, suspicion or disrespect here. In a climate of compassion, there are no power struggles, no secrets and no manipulation. There is fortitude, desire, will, and humor.

Furthermore, souls generally distrust themselves—not each other. Souls can make cynical remarks but without resentment or jealousy—without bodies, souls take criticism in a non-personal, less emotionally charged way. They are infused with energy by their group and by their Guides. Above and surrounding each group is a bright cylindrical cone. The top funnels energy down like a waterfall, spreading a circle of energy that allows the souls to concentrate on their mental sameness as a group. There is a feeling of the souls' thoughts being expanded—then drawn up and returned back with more knowledge added.

Souls within their cluster groups have a close relationship with each other based on their previous incarnations. "Members of the same cluster group are closely united for all eternity. These tightly-knit clusters are often composed of like-minded souls with common objectives which they continually work out with each other. Usually they choose lives together as relatives and close friends during their incarnations on Earth" (Newton, *Journey of Souls*, p. 88). Souls can theoretically meet up with souls who belong in other cluster groups, but they usually do not socialize with them. It is more common for one to interact primarily within its own cluster group.

Step 27: Council of Elders

After having had a chance to greet friends in the soul group, the Guide takes the soul to the Council, a group of wise Beings. The Guide stands behind and to the left of the soul in the room. Sometimes the Guide speaks on behalf of the soul. The Council evaluates the soul's perceptions of the most recent life lived and how it could have done better, and what good things it accomplished. The soul can freely express itself and any frustrations or special requests. Because each of the Council members has a specialty, he asks his questions accordingly (Newton, *Journey of Souls*, pp. 85–86). Souls are treated fairly by the Council; in return souls feel reverence toward them.

"Souls who come before their respective Councils have been debriefed during orientation sessions with their Guides. However, it is in front of the Council where souls feel most vulnerable about their past performance" (Newton, *Destiny of Souls*, p. 210). The object of the meeting is not to demean the soul or to punish him for his shortcomings. The Council's purpose is to (firmly, but benevolently) question the soul in order to help it achieve its goals in the next lifetime. Here is an inside look into a typical meeting:

> The Elders ask how we feel about major episodes in our life and our courses of action. Desirable actions and those that were counterproductive are discussed openly without acrimony... Regardless of the number of times we continue to make mistakes, the Council has enormous patience... If the Council... were not so indulgent, the average soul would simply give up and not come back to Earth. Souls have the right of refusal to return to Earth. The Elders probe for answers of how we think our host body served or hindered de-

velopment. The Council is already considering our next potential body and future environment. They wish to know how we feel about another incarnation... The Council is not so concerned with how many times we fell down in our progress through life, but whether we had the courage to pick ourselves up and finish strong (Newton, *Destiny of Souls*, p. 211).

At the end of the encounter, the Council members tell the Guide that they want to see the soul for a second time just before it decides to incarnate again.

Step 28: Return to Cluster Group

The soul then returns to its cluster group and finally feels that it has arrived home. After an eventful journey, it will now begin the process of learning and evaluating the life that just ended. In order to purify itself from indiscretions committed, the soul will proceed to gehinom.

Step 29: Gehinom

Dante Alighieri wrote that "the hottest places in Hell are reserved for those who, in times of great moral crisis, maintain their neutrality."

There may be truth in this, but the Jewish idea of gehenna (gehinom) is not equivalent to most conceptions of hell. Rather it is more of a purgatory where the soul is purged from all defilement it has accumulated during its life on Earth. This purgatory is often described in lurid physical details of fire and cold, yet the rabbis warn against seeing gehenna as a material entity. It is rather like the pain of anxiety intensified by silence and a deep awareness of the evil committed. Curiously, according to tradition, gehenna is emptied on the Sabbath. Some claim that this respite is granted only to those who had kept the Sabbath in their lives. Others disagree, claiming that gehenna is emptied for all; were it not for the weekly bliss and light that the Sabbath provides, the soul would be unable to endure the anguish of gehenna (Schacter, see note 19).

Judaism does not teach about heaven and hell like in other faiths. There is no lake of fire, no eternal condemnation for those who do wrong. The Talmud (Eruvin 19) tells us there are three openings from which to gain entry—in the desert, sea, and Jerusalem. The maximum time one spends there is about 12 months (Talmud, Shabbat 33b). During that time you are shown what your life was and what it could have been had you lived up to your full potential. These images show you not just yourself, but all the ways your choices affected those around you. It is said that it is not the first set of images, but rather the second set which is the most difficult to watch, as we see what we could have been. And it is through this process that we are purified and then may enter into paradise.[12]

Gehinom has a divine but blinding light. The source of suffering here is that through one's actions in life, he enclothes himself in darkness. Once confronted with this reality, the contrast is too much to bear (Winkler, *Dybbuk*, p. 77). Those who don't make it to gehinom (i.e., suicides) are driven by two angels in aimless wandering across the face of the Earth until they are ready to accept responsibility for their actions, at which point they are granted entry to gehinom. They will accompany the soul at all times except for Shabbat (ibid., p. 78).

Gehinom Defined

The "fires of hell" are a metaphor[13] for a place of intense embarrassment and frustration. The more one is preoccupied with excessive material yearnings in this world, the more the soul will undergo withdrawal symptoms during the painful purification process (Winkler, *Dybbuk*, pp. 285–286).

Gehinom is fairly well defined in rabbinic literature. It is sometimes translated as "hell," but the Christian version of hell is different from the Jewish view of gehinom. Some Christians believe that Hell is an abode of eternal torment where sinners go, and is also for anyone who does not accept Jesus as their messiah and God. Other Christians believe Hell is a place of separation from God from which believers are eventually saved by Jesus. Roman Catholics believe that Hell is a place of eternal suffering — physical, mental and spiritual suffering. Roman Catholics also have a notion of Purgatory as a place for souls who are truly repentant and can return to God once it is purged of its sins. Purgatory can last a day or thousands of years depending on the amount of cleansing the individual soul requires.

For Jews, gehinom—while certainly a terribly unpleasant place—is not hell. It is a spiritual forge where the soul is purified for its eventual ascent to Gan Eden [Heaven], and where all imperfections are purged. In this sense, it is somewhat similar to the Roman Catholic purgatory; however the time period has a definite limit.

Lori Palatnik in *A Jewish Understanding of Life After Death* describes *gehinom* as a hospital for the soul. We do not want to go there, but it is good to know it is there. God created this location as a *chesed*, or kindness. It is a place where one feels extreme shame for what he could have accomplished, but didn't.

As for the question of purgatory, again, there is no one Jewish position on the subject, even if we limit ourselves to the traditional Orthodox position. The Zohar (Vayechi, Folio 238b) mentions that the period of judgment is 12 months, where half the time is spent in fire for not adhering to prohibitions. The other half is spent in the snow for laziness and turning a cold shoulder toward the fulfillment of mitzvot. Moreover, with specific regard to the wicked, between purification for each sin, the soul is raised out of gehinom and rests briefly in lower Gan Eden according to what it deserves from the specific purification. However, it is again sent to gehinom to face the punishment of its next sin. It is first announced for all to hear, as the Targum, a biblical commentary (Ecclesiastes 12:14), says: "In the end all will be heard, even those sins that were performed in a hidden place. This causes great embarrassment to the soul" (Zohar Chaye Sara, Folio 130b).

Each category of sin, depending on its severity, is handled by different courts. The Talmud refers to the deceased going to a World of Truth or going to the heavens—without distinction. It is generally assumed these are synonyms, but these quotes still speak of a single afterlife. Others speak of the Garden of Eden and gehinom. Neither could be meant literally, as Adam was in the literal Garden before death, and the valley of Hinnom is a valley in Jerusalem where the Canaanite locals practiced human sacrifice by passing their children through the fires for Molech, an ancient Phoenician and Ammonite god. Some therefore understand this to mean that Eden vs. gehinom is not a difference in "location" but rather a difference in how one experiences the afterlife. Someone who spent life developing an appreciation for God and truth will find it as pleasant (Heb: Eden) as the garden; those who developed interests in other pursuits will find the experience hellish.

A number of sources, such as Rabbi Chaim of Vilozhin, founder of the current Yeshiva movement in the late eighteenth/early nineteenth century, and Rabbi Israel of Salant, founder of the Mussar movement (late eighteenth century) each describe the fires of gehinom as those of shame. For example, the Talmud tells us that the number of people subject to a permanent "stay" in gehinom is very small. These are people who outright reject the Torah's claim that an afterlife exists. The Talmud (Sanhedrin 105) names four commoners (Bilam, Doeg, Achitophel, Gechazi) who qualified as a result of their intransigence on this issue. For these few people, they identified themselves with sin to such an extent that abandoning sin would essentially mean abandoning their essence.[14]

Yet there are other descriptions of gehinom (Reisheet Chochma, Shaar Hayir'a, Chapters 13:5, 26). It is a place that has seven levels—one below another—each corresponding to the seven types of evildoers: *rah* (inherently evil), *bliyaal* (worthless), *choteh* (willful sinner), *rasha* (wicked), *mashchit* (destructive), *letz* (scorner), *yahir* (condescending). In each residence there is an angel in charge under the general supervision of Dumah, the angel responsible of all gehinom. There are angels of destruction under the angel in charge who mete out judgment to each evildoer individually.

The following (abridged) description of the seven levels comes from the Zohar (Pekudei, Folio 263):

Bor: For those who were engaged in wasteful conversations and showed lack of respect toward talmidei chachamim.

When a soul reaches the first *heichal* of *kedusha* (Temple of Holiness) in lower Gan Eden, the angel Tahriel stands by the gate, and if the soul is not yet worthy to enter, he pushes the soul outside where it is scooped up by the angel Dumah and is led to the first temple of impurity called "bor." Patot is the angel in charge here and he stands on the grave at the time the body is judged at which time he shatters the eyes of the body because this angel earned its right to own it by having succeeded in luring man into utilizing his eyes for impure thoughts. In this temple there are angels of destruction in the image of snakes and scorpions who bite and sting the soul.

Shachat: Green fire and darkness. Souls who arrive here are those who embarrassed another in public, were proud, rejoiced in the evildoing of his friend, did not appear in a place of worship, showed no niceties toward another, or cursed another with derisive laughter until the victim reached embarrassment.

It is totally dark here (indicating that the punishments meted out are of the highest severity) and there are three windows. These windows contain those who spilled their seed in many different ways and those who had illicit relations. Thousands of angels of destruction stand ready to punish and render the soul impure. In this section reside all the secrets of witchery utilized to kill man before his time. From here also emanate angels of destruction who come down to this world to flip good dreams into lies.

Dumah (avadon): Those who are foul-mouthed individuals, speakers of *lashon hara* (communicating derogatory or damaging information), those who do not give another the benefit of the doubt, lend money with interest, don't answer "amen," and put down another will surely reach this level. Dumah also happens to be the name of the minister who is in charge of overseeing gehinom. He is also known as the angel of death (Zohar Chaye Sara, Folio 121). He presides over Samriel, appointed to man the gates of gehinom.

There are four windows here. In the first, angels of destruction strike and weaken those who walked alone and acted untruthfully.

The second is where the notes are gathered and passed along to the angels of destruction with specific instructions on how to carry out the punishments. The third contains those who suffered from various sicknesses (*kadachat*). The fourth is where the spirit responsible for the death of children resides. This particular spirit appears to be playing with the children and gives off a maternal aura, but this is how the angel gets close enough to ultimately take their souls. Here also reside those who scoffed at the Torah and those who did not guard their tongue.

Teet Hayaven: This level is designated for those who answer the poor and the downtrodden with contempt, masturbators, one who has sexual relations with a *nidda* (a menstruating woman), and one who takes a bribe.

This is where the scale is weighed at Rosh Hashana. There are evil spirits here who succeeded in luring man into coveting women and causing failure to guard one's tongue. Also included here are those who didn't observe the Shabbat with good food and those who used foul language.

Sheol: Those who reach this level are non-believers in the Torah and in the Resurrection. Souls who come here brought enmity and hatefulness to the world. They were men who drew others into fights[15], didn't do *chesed* when they had the opportunity, didn't circumcise their sons, and did not fear God.

Tzalmavet: Those who succumbed to having had illicit and carnal relations.

Within this level is a sub-level called Beit Chaver, in which there are four windows that contain those who engaged in wrongful kissing, those who were entrapped by a harlot, and fools. The neshama leaves the body with pain and difficulty. Here reside those who were brazen, boastful, foul-mouthed, haughty and rude. Angels of destruction from here turn dreams of future events into rubble.

Arka: The fire of *gehinom* and the snow called *Tzalmon* are here. Also those who caused sorrow to others reside here.

In each of the above levels there is a corresponding door leading sideways to lower Gan Eden (Chesed L'Avraham, p. 238). Based on what is reported in the Zohar (Vaera, Folio 28—Tosefta), this means that since gehinom is reported to be north of the "yishuv" (Israel, the center of the world) and lower Gan Eden via Hebron is located to the south of Jerusalem, then the corresponding doors leading sideways are on gehinom's southern end (see Figure 1).

As noted, each of the above levels has a gate outside with someone in charge. Every Shabbat these internal gates open up and the wicked step out to the outer gate of gehinom and meet other souls who await their next journey after having been purified in gehinom.

Another place in gehinom is called "hot dung." It is called this due to the refuse that is left over from the purification process. Those who are judged here caused many other people to sin. Also here are the wicked who were stubborn and did not regret their actions before their death, as well as those who willfully initiate the spilling of their semen. They remain here for generations (Zohar Terumah, Folio 150b). Some say this place is actually located in the Teet Hayaven level described above.

A stark example of what happens in *shachat* (see above—the place a person ends up who embarrassed someone in public) is that souls are taken every Shabbat eve to two snow-covered mountains and left there until Saturday night, at which time they are pushed to their spot in gehinom with snow placed under their armpits in order to freeze them during the course of the week.

Bor is composed of fire and coal in the shape of a mountain upon which the wicked are placed. The Talmud in three separate places (Tractates Shabbat 33, Rosh Hashana 17, and Eduyot 2) states that the soul's ashes are spread at the feet of the righteous, after which they are returned to their regular form and leave gehinom with blackened faces to admit to their embarrassment. This section of hell is the least stringent among the seven.

The Minchat Yehuda (p. 184) lists a number of indiscretions and the recommended amount of days one is to fast in order to mitigate the suffering one might otherwise endure as a cleansing agent. For example, for showing disrespect to parents, one should fast for 45 days (not in a row—this could be over time). These fast days are designed to lessen the purification process in gehinom.

Depending upon the level of spirituality one attains during his lifetime, he will remain in gehinom accordingly. There are those who need a mere rinsing of some stains from his clothes while others need bleaching (Nishmat Chaim, Article II:23).

One can be spared from harsh judgment by bringing to the next world accrued Torah knowledge and good deeds, plus the experience of having suffered in this world. Thus, the truly righteous may only need to make a cameo appearance here or if they perished through an act of sanctifying His name, may skip this station altogether.

Why would a soul choose to suffer the awful experiences of gehinom, described above, when he could instead decide to do another gilgul? Because there are no guarantees. The anguish of another gilgul could be worse than gehinom itself (Reisheet Chochma, Shaar Hayir'a, Chapter 13:80; Zohar Mishpatim 94). When one thinks

about all of the trials and tribulations of beginning and then enduring another life, with no real certainty that he will even attain his
objective and targeted tikkun, it quickly becomes an overwhelming
prospect. Others, however, may choose to take this route because
of the concomitant rewards and pleasures. Moreover, according to
Rabbi Avraham Azulai (Chesed L'Avraham, p. 196), not every tikkun
can be accomplished by going through gehinom. There are those tikkunim that can only be accomplished via a gilgul, for example, one
who was missing a limb in a previous life and therefore was not able
to perform the *mitzvah* of donning tefillin. Not fulfilling all of the
248 positive commandments is another reason for doing a gilgul. The
idea is to complete them. Gehinom is usually reserved for cleansing
a transgression of any of the 365 negative commandments.

Nonetheless, it is important to note here that a soul has the
opportunity to do a make-up exam if he failed in his first life. If he
performed the positive mitzvot correctly, but not perfectly, he is not
obligated to do another gilgul in order to attain perfection, but the
choice is left up to the individual soul.

Upon completion of the purification process, God will begin
to raise the soul in preparation for its departure from gehinom.
The soul sits by the gate of gehinom and upon seeing an incoming
wicked soul entering and being judged, the soul asks for mercy upon
him, having just gone through the same process. When God sees
how the soul went out of his way to help another, He grants the soul
further merit by accelerating his path to the next stage (Zohar Vayera, Folio 108). By contrast the souls of the wicked who were sent
down to Sheol can only be extricated by righteous souls who pass by
gehinom on their way to lower Gan Eden. Only they can raise these
souls (Zohar Lech Lecha, Folio 77b; Zohar Pinchas, Folio 220) and
escort them out. The Vilna Gaon explains (based on Proverbs 13:8)

that the righteous must pass through gehinom on their way to the lower Gan Eden, but the "fires" do not affect them, as mentioned earlier in step 23.

Three types of people do not see even the facade of gehinom because the misery they suffer in this world atones for their sins. These include those who endure the exactions of poverty, suffer from intestinal disorders, and are traumatized by the pursuit of creditors. Some say even someone who tolerated a nasty wife is exempted (Talmud, Eruvin, 41b).

It is my understanding from speaking to a number of kabalists, that the very harsh descriptions in this section are mostly reserved for the truly wicked. For the rest of us, the regular life review, an integral part of gehinom, would be the next logical step, because it is a place of cleansing stains rather than a place of severe punishment.

Step 30: Life Review

Many souls skip the harshest sections of gehinom and arrive at the life review directly after the cluster group (Step 28). The wicked souls who did go through the intense purification process in gehinom will also arrive at the life review wing for further analysis of their immediate past life.

The soul comes to a round domed chamber with corridors going off in six directions. Small classrooms are located here for personal consultation. Each classroom is offset in such a way that no two classrooms face each other (Newton, *Destiny of Souls* p. 144) for maximum privacy.

The soul is then brought (by either his Guide or someone from his cluster group) to a large library. In this library, everything a soul sees is in live, miniature, and multi-dimensional pictures. There are long tables and thick books laid out before him. As mentioned in the Hagahot Mahartza commentary to the Talmud's Tractate Kedushin, "on man's activities one need not testify, for all is written in the book." The soul's past lives and alternatives to those lives—theoretical paths he could have taken had he made different choices—are available for viewing. Just as the person sat and learned from books when in this world, so too will the soul be "accustomed" to learning in this library (Maavar Yabok, Siftei Renanot, Chapter 25; Zohar Vayechi, Folio 227). Some of the questions posed to the soul include:

1 Did you deal faithfully in business?
2 Did you set aside times to study Torah?
3 Did you engage in procreation?
4 Did you look forward to/anticipate the redemption?
5 Did you engage in deepening your knowledge?
6 Did you try to deduce one thing from another?

(Shabbat 31a)

Moreover, cruelty—mental or physical against humans or animals—is highly karmic and is never justified. It is guaranteed that those who consistently abuse and harass others will have to face their victims in the afterlife before severest retribution. After the severest retribution of those who intentionally harassed and deliberately violated other peoples' rights, the transgressors will have to apologize and seek forgiveness from their victims before they are allowed to make any progress (Victor Zammit, *A Lawyer Presents the Case for the Afterlife*).

Future lives can be viewed as well, but only in small chunks.[16] As alluded to in an earlier chapter, this is due to the fact that a soul, exposed to knowing his future, could fail to make a concerted effort when incarnated again. Also, the future is not guaranteed as free will and other circumstances can change the picture radically. At this point in the library the emphasis is on the past and what lessons can be learned (as opposed to a visit to the Ring of Destiny, Step 36). Members of the soul group help one another go over mistakes and discuss the value of choices made—some humor and even teasing can occur. Souls love to tease and use humor in their groups but always show respect for one another. More than forgiveness, souls exercise tolerance (Newton, *Destiny of Souls*, p. 191).

The Guide is also around for help as needed and for individual counseling. We are not evaluated after death by our religious associations but rather by our conduct and values. "If traditional religious activity serves your purpose and provides you with spiritual sustenance, you are probably motivated by a belief in scripture and perhaps the desire for comradeship in worship," says Newton. But this pathway does not suit everyone. Similarly we are measured more by what we do for others (Newton, *Destiny of Souls*, p. 398). Charity saves one from death and the prayers of the poor are more accepted by God than the prayers of others (Zohar Beshalach, Folio 61, 61b). Why is the latter so? A poor person has no fear of physical retribution because during his lifetime his body is like a broken vessel. Hence, God has a natural affinity and closeness to the poor man's nefesh and will thus more readily accept his prayers.

Another way of looking at this life review is as follows:

Souls who come to Earth think of themselves as actors on a world stage, as Shakespeare wrote. When souls return to their cluster group after a particularly hard life, there are applause and shouts of "bravo." The applause is for a job well done at the end of the last act of the play of life. The Guides are stage directors who go over past life scenes with the souls frame by frame. Errors in judgment are presented in small doses. All possible outcomes are studied and compared by designing new scripts for these scenes with different sets of choices that could have been made in each circumstance. Behavioral patterns are minutely dissected with each soul playing a part—souls might even decide to switch roles. Souls gain perspective from being witness to their own past performance through other actors (ibid., p. 193).

The soul also can take time to go to the "rooms of recreation." Here they can meld their energy into animate and inanimate objects created for learning and pleasure. For example, a soul can think of what it wants to be and then be that thing (trees for serenity, butterflies for freedom, whales for power and immensity). Souls can also become amorphous without substance or texture and integrate into a particular feeling such as compassion in order to sharpen their sensitivity. Energy manipulation is a major part of a soul's training.

Step 31: River of Fire (*Nahar d'Nur*)

This is located in the northern-most part of gehinom. Literally translated from the Hebrew Nahar d'Nur, its contents are created from the perspiration of celestial beings that flows as they carry the Almighty's Seat of Glory and sing. According to Rav Zutra ben Tuvia (prominent student of the famous Babylonian Talmudist Rav Abba bar Ibo, circa 200 CE), the waters thereof are deposited onto the heads of the wicked in the third level of gehinom. Rav Shmuel, on the other hand, stated that heavenly hosts are created daily from this river and that it is in fact not a place of punishment for the wicked.

Nachmanides in Shaar Hagmul says that the fire is not like fire as we know it today. It emanates directly from under the Holy Throne.

For those who were killed *"al Kiddush Hashem,"* sanctifying God's name, it will not be necessary to purify themselves in this river. A spirit by the name of Tzadkiel accompanies the righteous to the river in order to bathe and undergo purification.

When a soul is ready to enter Gan Eden, it must first be immersed in this River of Fire (some call it River of Light), in order to empty the soul of any lingering Earth images so that it may, without further illusion, see heaven for what it really is. He is purged from the sins of commission in this world plus for those of omission. He is healed from the burns of its fire by virtue of a southerly wind of chesed that rejuvenates him (Zohar Pekudei, Folio 245).

The Gra (Rabbi Eliyahu, The Gaon of Vilna) holds that this stage takes place for a second time just before entering the upper Gan Eden (Even Shlayma 10:16). He describes therein four types of immersion (ibid., 10:17):

A The righteous are immersed in cold water.
B The wicked are immersed in fire.
C The "middle-of-the-roaders" are immersed in water plus fire, or hot water.
D The excessively wicked go to oblivion and are lost forever.

Upon this cleansing process, one's dirty clothes are removed and is then clad with new ones. At this point the angel Michael sacrifices the soul to God. This sacrifice, however, is not in the same sense as ritual slaughter of an animal. It is a vehicle through which the soul gets closer to God in order to bask in His glorious abundance, thereby elevating the soul further.

Step 32: Tunnel at the Cave of the Patriarchs

After Nahar d'Nur, the soul enters into the Cave of the Patriarchs (Mearat Hamachpelah) in the Israeli city of Hevron, which is the pathway leading to lower *Gan Eden* (Zohar Vayechi, Folio 219). Incidentally, those individuals who had an NDE describe a tunnel through which they proceed toward a bright light—this tunnel is thought to be the Cave of the Patriarchs (see Figure 1). Those who enter the Gateway (Step 13) also report going through a tunnel, but that seems to me to be a different one than the Cave of the Patriarchs. This is not altogether clear. Further, one may wonder how it is possible to be going through a tunnel that is physically located in Hevron when the soul has seemingly already made its way up to a different plane. The significance of this question may in part be answered by the account in Step 14, where the soul is reported to be moving across rather than up. Moreover, the theories (as explained in Step 33) of where lower Gan Eden is actually located may also give some hint to the possibility that this tunnel indeed extends from the city of Hevron.

One theory is that lower Gan Eden is located near the Cave as referenced by the forefather Jacob who commanded his sons to bury him only in the Cave because he knew of its proximity to lower Gan Eden—and because Adam was buried there as well (Zohar Vayechi, Folio 248b).

Within the Cave of the Patriarchs is a large hall where the tombs of the forefather Isaac and his wife Rebecca are located. Their burial place is somewhere below ground level of this hall, though its exact whereabouts is unknown. What is known is that in this hall there is a small cave below within which there is believed to be the portal to lower Gan Eden.

In the summer of 2009 I went on a tour of biblical Hevron and to The Cave of the Patriarchs and learned many new things about the holiness of the Cave itself. The tour guide, Rabbi Simcha Hochbaum, who is also a resident of Hevron, told us a story about his then seven-year old autistic son who, though non-verbal at the time, manifested a special curiosity about what was behind a particular set of doors in the Cave. It was forbidden to go there except by arrangement with the army (noted scholar Rabbi Moshe Yaakov claims that this is the very same hall where Isaac and Rebecca [Yitzchak and Rivka] are buried). One day his son somehow managed to get through to the other side and immediately came upon a smaller cave. He stopped at its opening and began flapping his arms and squealing with excitement. A number of soldiers spotted him and tried to pry him away from the site, but couldn't. They tracked down his father and summoned him to come right away to get his son. When the father arrived, he sat down next to his son and asked what led him to this particular location.

Up until this point in the youth's life, he had not uttered a word—he just made sounds. The youth then pointed down to the hole in the cave and said in a very clear voice, "Abba bayit, ima bayit, ohr po"—loosely translated as "Father's house, mother's house—there is light here." The father understood what his son was telling him—that Mearat HaMachepela is believed to be located very close to the opening of lower Gan Eden, based on a Zoharic reference to Adam and Eve being buried there. We also learned from the Zohar that all souls pass through this opening in their transition from this world to the next. How interesting it was to hear the vision of this youth who, like others coping with autism, has channels open to him that the general population does not.

Apropos of the above, the reader will note that in Figure 1 lower Gan Eden is shown as being northwest of The Cave of the Patriarchs. The youth in the above story was reported to have pointed southerly from the Cave from which emanated a light. If we are to believe that that is the opening to lower Gan Eden, then how could it be depicted as northwest of the Cave?

One possibility is that this location serves as a portal, allowing practical, rapid travel between two distant locations. What is important to understand here is that once one enters a portal, he may be transported to another dimension or plane that is not necessarily in juxtaposition to the portal's locus. The youth may have pointed downward to the light, but in fact if one were to actually enter that portal, he could theoretically end up northwest of the Cave.

An archeological reference that came close to pinpointing the exact location of the portal to Gan Eden was discovered 20 years ago by Rabbi Moshe Yaakov. He was the first to descend to the level of the actual graves of the Patriarchs and report his findings. The structure of the building that now stands was originally built by King David during the seven-year period he reigned as king in Hebron. Beneath the structure lie the graves of our forefathers and their wives. The location in the Isaac and Rebecca Hall, from which the youth pointed, is the exact spot that Rabbi Yaakov commenced his journey down fifteen steps and then to a lower level where he discovered the graves of Adam and Eve, Abraham and Sarah, Isaac and Rebecca, Jacob and Leah, and Moses and Tzipporah. He reported smelling sweet incense by the graves of Adam and Eve and feeling a distinct wind from the direction of the grave of Isaac and Rebecca. The entire area, situated from the southwest point of the structure going northwesterly, is where the portal to Gan Eden is reported to be according to sources in the Zohar, and is consistent with these findings.

The following is a summarized description of Gan Eden as told by Rabbi Abba to Rabbi Elazar, son of Rabbi Shimon bar Yochai (Zohar Omissions, Folio 303b):

The righteous souls see Adam sitting by the gates of Gan Eden looking upon others who have followed the ways of the Torah, and he is happy among them. (Although in Medrash Tanchuma Parshat Chukat it says that the righteous say to Adam "you are responsible for death in olam hazeh"). Then those on their way to Gan Eden come close to the outer wall (among 3 walls) that surrounds the Gan. The Minister Yazriel acts as the Guide. The souls still do not enter Gan Eden but rather come upon a gate of gehinom first and the minister calls out "cool down the smoke and fire"—whereupon the righteous come through, dip quickly in Nahar d'Nur and exit. They then reach the gate of lower Gan Eden and the minister announces: "Open the gates so that the righteous, who are the guardians of our faith, may enter." They enter and there is great happiness. Beautiful grass, springs of water gushing from all sides, and many trees can be seen. For three days they are hidden within temples whereupon they come out to the courtyard of Gan Eden where a holy gust of wind is blowing and thus each inherits his own estate. Above all this, a horizon opens and fills the Gan with the splendor of God and all the righteous souls are illuminated by it.

Step 33: Lower Gan Eden

Many theories have been put forth regarding the location of this paradise. The Zohar (Lech Lecha, Folio 81) tells us that lower Gan Eden has many of the structural forms of this world and similar landscapes to upper Gan Eden. So, lower Gan Eden is very much a combination of both. The special clothing worn here comes to the soul as a result of his actions on Earth, and the clothing of the upper Gan Eden comes from the soul's thoughts, will, and heart's intent when immersed in learning or in prayer.[17]

Near the Equator

One source tells us that lower Gan Eden is actually on Earth's plane below the equator where the day remains 12 hours long (Shaar Hagmul L'HaRamban, p. 324). The Maavar Yabok brings down the opinion of Rabbi Shimon bar Yochai (Rashbi), who says that it is along the Pacific Ocean near the equator, at the center of the world between a populated land and an unpopulated one, wherein there is a hidden locale not known to man. Jerusalem is said to be at the center of the populated land. Created on the third day of Creation, the ground of Gan Eden is not like the geological material of this world—rather it is comprised of a very pure substance (Tikunei HaZohar Introduction, Folio 17).

A spring comes forth from a pillar, where the waters spread out to the four corners of the world. In a text of questions and answers from nineteenth-century halachist and kabalist Rabbi Joseph Chaim ben Elijah al-Chakam[18] in the name of Rabbi Isaac Luria, it states that Gan Eden is located at the midpoint of the world's equator which is south of present day Israel.

Another opinion is brought forth by Pirkei D'Rabbi Eliezer (an aggadic-midrashic work) based on two sources in the Talmud (Bava Batra 84a; Brachot 55b) that lower Gan Eden is adjacent to Mount Moriah, the Temple Mount in Jerusalem (Har Habayit).

Some sources (The Talmud, Brachot 34b; Zohar Chadash Bereisheet, Folio 23) indicate that Gan and Eden are in fact two separate entities as it is written in Genesis 2:10 that four rivers (Pishon, Gihon, Chidekel, and Prat) emanate from Eden in order to water the garden (gan). There is an upper Eden and a lower Eden just as there is an upper Gan and a lower Gan. God planted lower Eden under upper Eden and lower Gan under upper Gan such that the river that emanates from upper Eden waters the upper Gan and the river from lower Eden waters the lower Gan. Forty-eight times a day drops of water from Eden fall into Gan, and this is the source of the rivers mentioned above (Zohar Chaye Sara, Folio 125 – Midrash Ne'elam). The drops of water emanating from Eden are likened to the spiritual abundance of pleasure. Thus, Gan and Eden are equals—Eden is situated above Gan, because Eden is in olam habriya and Gan is in olam ha'asiya.

God named Gan Eden a nut garden because it has a number of hard shell rings around it protecting its inner core (ibid.). Such is the composition of Eden—there are two worlds surrounding each other—olam ha'asiya and olam hayetzira, and in the innermost core is olam habriya. Hence, Gan Eden is named for the name of the place and for its source.

The Ramban (Nachmanides) brings forth his own opinion, stating that Gan Eden sits somewhere east of India. The proof he brings from a number of different sources (Shaar Hagmul L'HaRamban, p. 325) tells the story of Ascalpinus of Macedonia who, along with forty men well versed in medicine, traveled to a place east of Eden (along The Prat River north) in order to search for medicinal tree leaves, and also for the Tree of Life. When they approached the entrance to *Gan Eden* (within half a mile according to Maavar Yabok, Siftei Renanot, Chapter 33), they were all burned by a bolt of fire from a revolving sword that is stationed at the entrance in order to prevent individuals from entering. There were no survivors. The

Ramban claims this was known throughout the lands in the Far East.

The Rambam (Maimonides) takes exception to this and states that Gan Eden will be revealed to us by God at some point in the future. Furthermore, the commentary Chazon Yoel (ibid., p. 327, note 633) claims that the Ramban's version is difficult to accept because he brings, as stated above, the source that Gan Eden is adjacent to The Temple Mount. If so, how could it be in the Far East? In Tractate Eruvin 19a Reish Lakish questions whether the entrance to Gan Eden is in the city of Beit Shean in Israel or whether it is outside of Israel but in the general region. More modern attempts at theorizing its location place it somewhere in Egypt, Turkey, India or even Ethiopia.

And finally, in juxtaposition to gehinom which is in the north, lower Gan Eden lies in the southwest section of the world (Even Shlayma 10:27). It was created 1,368 years before the world, and is 60 times its size (Chesed L'Avraham, p. 237). The Talmud, (Taanit 10) however, says that there are those who say that there is no size limitation to gehinom, whereas others say that Gan Eden has no limit. The ground distance between this world and lower Gan Eden is one tefach (.0762 meters, or approximately three inches), and its juxtaposition is as follows: the northern edge of this world is one tefach away from the southern edge of lower Gan Eden (see Figure 1), and the form of "this world" (*olam hazeh*) is in the shape of the written form of the Hebrew letter "bet" (ב).

The Approach from the Outer Walls

As a soul approaches Gan Eden from its perimeter, it encounters three walls of fire (Tractate Seder Gan Eden). The outer wall is surrounded by black fire with a twirling sword revolving around its perimeter on a constant basis. There are four openings to this wall, with a distance of 120 amot (cubits) between them. The Angel Azriel is in charge here, mostly to save newly arrived righteous gentiles, converts to Judaism, and gentile leaders from Angels of Destruction who attempt to shove them back to gehinom.

The middle wall, whose distance from the outer wall is 600 cubits, is where souls gather from gehinom. This wall has a green and red fire surrounding it. The Angel Pniel is in charge. The light from the righteous shines upon these souls for a moment and then recedes. The heaven just above lower Gan Eden begins to rotate and the letters of God's name glisten as they charge up and down with a voice proclaiming "how good is your lot for having merited this," followed by melodious music.

The third wall appears as light and darkness mixed together and is the innermost wall of lower Gan Eden. Here the soul gets clothed in pure and holy robes (ibid.) and looks as it did on Earth. The soul can greet and recognize others who arrived there as well (see below for a more in-depth description). The Zohar (Shemot 13b) adds that when the soul arrives it is greeted by groups of other souls whereupon the newly arrived soul commences singing with the same kind of happiness it experienced on its wedding day.

On Shabbat one can see the *asseret harugei malchut* (the ten martyrs), *roshei yeshiva* (headmasters), and Moshe Rabbeinu's *yeshiva*. On the northern end there are seven houses containing righteous women such as Yocheved, Miriam, Avigail, Sara, Rivka, Rachel, and Leah.

Gender Differences

Rabbi Shimon was once asked if women are permitted to enter the yeshiva in Gan Eden where the righteous merit learning.

He answered: In a vision I was shown six temples in front of which stood a curtain, beyond which men were not permitted entrance. In these temples resided women prophets—and in a seventh one there were four more temples where the four matriarchs resided.

In Temple 1, Bitya, the daughter of Pharoah resides, along with Avigail, wife of King David and tens of thousands of righteous women. These women did not suffer in gehinom at all. Three times a day an announcement is put forth saying that the image of Moses is on its way, and when it comes near, Bitya bows down to him and says: "How fortunate am I to have witnessed the growth of this splendid light."

In Temple 2, Serach the daughter of Asher, resides along with Hulda and tens of thousands of other righteous women. Serach merited residing here because she notified Jacob that his son Joseph was still alive. Three times a day an announcement was put forth that the image of Joseph was arriving, and when it appears to her, she happily bows to him proclaiming: "How fortunate was I to have brought the news to your father Jacob that you were indeed alive."

In Temple 3 Yocheved and Miriam reside. All of the women here sing the Shirat Hayam (prayer recited in praise of the miracle of the splitting of the sea) every day, and Miriam also sings by herself, whereupon all of the righteous men listen to the praise coming out of her melodious voice.

For those wondering whether there is an issue of *kol isha*, the prohibition of a man listening to a woman sing because her voice is pleasant and therefore a temptation, there is not a problem. In Gan Eden souls are abstract beings [unclothed, bare, and disembodied] and there is no concept of a yetzer hara (evil inclination).

In Temple 4 Devora resides. She also sings on a daily basis.

Temple 5 is Chana's domain.

Temple 6 is Esther's domain.

(Descriptions of Temples 5 and 6 were omitted in the Zoharic text, Shlach, Folios 167, 167b).

All of these personalities retained the likeness of their original (physical) form in this world, and are clad in a spiritual light similar to the righteous males, as a result of their performance of mitzvot in this world. The only difference is that they do not emanate as bright a light as the males because women are exempt from performing *mitzvot asei shehazman grama* (positive commandments that are time-dependent).

Neshamot here enjoy spiritual pleasures but still have a spiritual body resembling their former bodies (as opposed to upper Gan Eden where souls do not have any spiritual image resembling their former bodies). The spiritual body is not as meaty or "thick-muscled" as we have come to know it in this world. The fruit is also not as thick as we know it in this world, but much thinner and fine—almost like air.

Visits to Upper Gan Eden

All day the male and female souls are separate and each night they come together with their respective soulmates. Just as on Earth couples come together body to body, in the next world they come together light to light. On Shabbat and on Rosh Chodesh (when the new moon appears) only the males ascend to upper Gan Eden, receive new nuances on the Torah, and return to lower Gan Eden to further discuss these Torah thoughts with their yeshiva headmaster (Zohar Shlach, Folio 167, 167b).

What, then, do the women do when the males go to upper Gan Eden? They come out of their respective temples and proceed to gather in each other's temples.

Every seventh year, when the lights of all seven emanations are at its peak, an announcement is made for all the men and women of Gan Eden to gather round, whereupon all will merit ascending from lower Gan Eden to upper Gan Eden, and all the children enter the yeshiva of the angel Metatron. It is said there is no greater happiness than to witness this sight (ibid., Folio 171b).

Clothing, Fragrances, Tree of Life

It is a difficult trek to go from Earth to lower Gan Eden due to Angels of Destruction stationed on the path in between. Therefore, God made piles of earth (as in dirt) on each side of the Cave of the Patriarchs (which connects Earth to lower Gan Eden) stretching from Hebron to lower Gan Eden in order that the souls can pass through directly and not be harmed by these destructive angels (ibid.).

After the immersion in the Nahar d'Nur, a righteous soul making his way to lower Gan Eden will, along with two angels, escort the newly arrived souls to the gate of lower Gan Eden and prepare them for their entrance by (the angels) proclaiming: "Here they are! Here are the souls who have been purified." The souls meet the angels called cruvim, who guard the entrance with a revolving sword of fire, and are then allowed entry (Reisheet Chochma, Shaar Hayir'a, 13:86-87 and Shaar Ahava, 6:57). The soul sees a celestial heaven in four shades of color (white, green, red, and black) with four openings. He sees the chariots of Michael and Refael, who proclaim, "Come in peace, come in peace." Then the chariots of Gavriel and Nuriel come down from two of the openings and hover above the soul, and from there proceed to a hidden chamber called "Ohalot," containing 12 different fragrances. The soul immerses itself in these spices. The soul is clad with special clothing according to his spiritual level and here all of the good deeds accomplished in his immediate past life are recorded and announced (Zohar Vayakhel as quoted in *Maavar Yabok*, new edition, p. 306).

More specifically, the soul is given seven kinds of clothes from the cloud of honor, with two crowns placed on his head (one made of fine stones and jewels, and the other of gold). He is given eight myrtles in his hand, whereupon he is commended and is invited to eat his bread in joy. He is then placed into a river surrounded by 800 kinds of myrtle, roses, and pine, where each soul has its own canopy. Near this river are four other rivers made up separately of milk, wine, persimmon, and honey. Above each canopy is a gold cluster embedded with 30 permanent jewels. Inside the canopy is a long gold table made up of fine stones and jewels as well. 600,000 angels proclaim to him: Eat of the honey and drink of the wine because you studied Torah in earnest (Tractate Gan Eden).

Further, there are 310 worlds in lower *Gan Eden* and no night. Each day God renews upon the soul four shifts in which he is made to be 1) a child (in order to be as happy as a child again), 2) a young person, 3) a middle-aged person, and 4) elderly. There are 80,000 types of trees—each of its four sides has the angels stationed and singing with their pleasant voices. The Tree of Life stands in the middle with 800 kinds of tastes, each with a unique fragrance and appearance. There are also seven clouds of honor above the soul—its fragrances filling the air. Sitting just below the soul are *talmidei chachamim* learning Torah (ibid.).

All this occurs 30 days after death, whereupon the *neshama* is shown its place (the nefesh and ruach are still undergoing their respective purification processes simultaneous to this).

Rabbi Chaim Vital gives his personal description of lower Gan Eden as it was revealed to him in a dream:

Gan Eden is described as an endlessly large courtyard with streaming rivers flowing therein. On the banks of the rivers are beautiful, robust, fresh fruit trees. Most are apple trees with the scent of myrrh and the twelve fragrances from the chamber called ohalot. Fifteen-hundred scents/fragrances emanate from lower Gan Eden every day and rise to upper Gan Eden. The trees are tall, its top branches bent over until they practically reach the ground, forming the appearance of a tabernacle. There are many white swans around and they are learning mishnayot from Tractate Shabbat. While they are walking they are learning, and at the end of each Mishna or perek (chapter), they would extend their necks and pluck an apple off of a tree, and then drink water from the river. I understood that these swans are the neshamot of the tzaddikim of the baalei Mishna, but I did not know why they looked like swans and not like people.

I then was led further into Gan Eden and saw a hill that was the height of a normal sized man which was opened from the west and a ladder with three stone steps to its entrance. I entered this place and saw The Almighty Himself, sitting on a chair on the south end of the room, and he looked like an elderly and highly distinguished gentleman, his beard as white as snow, with tzaddikim sitting on the ground laden with new and plush carpets before Him, learning Torah. When I saw His face I began to shake and I fell on my face between His feet. He placed His hand on my right side and said to me: "Chaim, My son, get up, why do you fall on your face—do not be afraid." I then said unto Him: "My Lord, after seeing You, I literally have no strength left to stand before You." Whereupon He said: "Here, I have now strengthened you—stand up and sit to My right where you see that vacant spot." Then I said to Him: "How can I sit there—it looks like Harav Yosef Karo has his eyes set on that spot!"

And He answered: "Yes, that's what I thought of originally, to have him sit there, but I assigned him another seat and this one I prepared for you." And I then said: "But this place was always reserved for Shmuel HaNavi z"l." And then He said: "True, it is his place, but ever since the Temple was destroyed, he took it upon himself to not sit here until the new future Temple is built. And meanwhile, he went off to Jerusalem to the place of the destroyed Temple, and there he stands always and mourns for it, until the new one will be built. Therefore, his seat is free, and I am assigning it to you." I then sat to His right, really close to Him with the tzaddikim who were already in their places (Rabbi Chaim Vital, *Sefer Hachezionot*, pp. 112–114).

The Seven *Heichalot*

There are many other classes and levels of righteous that dwell here with God sitting amongst them and learning Torah. These include:
- Those who perished to sanctify His name (i.e., Rabbi Akiva et al.)
- Those who drowned
- Rabbi Yochanan ben Zakai and students
- Baalei teshuva
- Bachelors who never tasted sin
- Modest scholars
- Educators of young children
- Those who raised children who learn Torah
- Communal leaders whose egos and pride did not interfere
- Givers of charity
- The poor and the converted
- Those who feared sin
- Those who performed acts of kindness
- Those who buried the dead

- Those who visited the sick
- Lenders to those in need
- Those who raised orphans
- Peacemakers
- Honorable kings

The above list is shown in various *heichalot* (temples) as follows. The soul passes through the seven heichalot in lower Gan Eden to experience the din, or judgment, that other souls endured. This gives the soul an appreciation and perspective of what it has merited in continuing on to the higher levels of heichalot in upper Gan Eden.

Heichal 1: *Livnat Sapir*—surrounded by high quality stone and gold. There is an opening to gehinom in order to view those who didn't merit this heichal. Three times during the day this heichal receives light from the sefira Tiferet. Here reside neshamot who underwent conversion. Ovadia the Prophet is in charge here. And the angel Rachmiel greets the neshamot of the converted.

Heichal 2: *Etzem HaShamayim*—Light of the Bina, or knowledge, shines through. Here reside neshamot that suffered torture in this world and those who say "Yehay shmay rabba..." with all their might. The angel Orpaniel is in charge here—he comforts all those who suffered and rejuvenates them by escorting souls to the River of d'Nur. Adiriel the angel cares for those who died by snake bites and for those who hardly tasted sin.

Heichal 3: *Noga*—Here reside neshamot who suffered serious illness, babies who died and those who mourned over the destruction of the Temple. The Mashiach comforts here too. The angel Ahinael is in charge of the babies who died and didn't have a chance to learn Torah in this world, so he stands over them and teaches them Torah.

Heichal 4: *Ahava*—here reside Neshamot who mourn Zion and Jerusalem and all those who were killed by other nations. The Mashiach cries but is comforted in upper Gan Eden and then comes down again. Here also reside the ten martyrs. The angel Gadrihael cares for those killed by other nations and stays with them until God avenges their murders.

Heichal 5: *Zechut*—residing here are *baalei teshuva*, those who sanctified God's name in death. Menashe King of Yehuda is the minister here. Complete *tzadikim* do not frequent here. The angel Adarhinael is responsible for those *baalei teshuva* who had intentions of repenting but died before they had a chance to see their intent through.

Heichal 6: *Ratzon*—those who always gave the benefit of the doubt to others with dedication. Avraham Avinu is the minister here—he stands on the right, Isaac on the left, Jacob in the middle and the twelve tribes stand surrounding him. Tzadkiel the angel cares for those baalei teshuva who made a complete return to God.

Heichal 7: *Kodesh Kadashim*—In upper Gan Eden. This Heichal is hidden from neshamot in heichalot beneath this one. In the middle there is a pillar adorned with three colors (black signifying gevura, white signifying chesed, and green signifying tiferet) with a ladder upon which neshamot climb from lower to upper Gan Eden. This pillar is called Machon Har Zion. Michael is the head minister over all the angels. Here reside neshamot of hasidim who reached the 50th level of Bina, where the soad (secret) of freedom exists.

Just as there are seven heichalot in lower Gan Eden, so too are seven in upper Gan Eden in order to provide tikkun to tzadikim. For a more detailed description of each Heichal, see Zohar Bereisheet Folios 38-45.

Emotional Bliss

The purpose of the soul entering a physical body is to purify it so that it is worthy of entering Gan Eden (Luzzato, *Daat Tevunot*, pp. 54–61). Thus the soul merits basking in the Divine light as its reward for its efforts in purifying the body. Each neshama wears a crown on its head according to its level of honor. It would bring shame to a soul to wear a crown it did not actually merit.

The houses in which they dwell are many miles long with one hundred angels serving in each. They dance and sing when the soul enters whereupon they clad him with eight silk robes. There is also reference to souls mating in lower Gan Eden.

The soul enters the lower Gan Eden, which is a paradise of emotional bliss. While on Earth, most persons are unable to experience more than one dominant emotion at a time. However, the bliss of the souls in the lower Gan Eden is likened to a majestic chord of emotions that the soul feels toward God and towards other souls. Pleasant voices reverberate. The sky above lower Gan Eden rotates twice every day in order that the righteous in every part of Gan Eden can see and take pleasure in the hidden treasures above (Zohar Vayakhel, Folio 210). In the Hasidic view, heaven is organized into societies (referred to as "soul groups" by Newton). Those souls who share mutual interests are drawn together so they can serve their Creator according to their own specialty and individuality. Each heavenly society is taught by its own rabbi (or guide) and led to further celestial attainments. The righteous appear here clad much in the same way they appeared on Earth and will recognize one another (Zohar Bereisheet, Folio 7). It will look like a body with 248 body parts. Over time this look will change to 248 mitzvot, and eventually to 248 spiritual lights (corresponding to the 248 positive commandments). Thus, beyond the physical beauty of lush grass, abundant fruit trees, and wondrous views and landscaping, lower Gan Eden is the heaven of emotional fervor. It is also called "*tsror hachayyim,*" where souls reside under the Seat of Glory (Shaar Hagmul, p. 352). When the soul is here it is considered an "honor" (*kavod*), as opposed to when the soul is in *gehinom,* where it is an "embarrassment."

Every Shabbat, *rosh chodesh,* and holidays the souls can go to a place called "*Chomot Yerushalayim,*" or the walls of Jerusalem. There they bow down and delight in the Creator's light, whereupon they return to their place in lower Gan Eden. They can then fly around the world (without fear of being caught by intruders since the Shabbat atmosphere is holy and contains no impurities) and look down upon those suffering in this world, and then appear before *Mashiach* to report on this suffering, whereupon Mashiach cries and evinces the mercy of the Almighty. The souls then return to their respective places (Maavar Yabok, Siftei Renanot, Chapter 37).

The Zohar (Mishpatim, Folio 97b) explains that on regular weekdays, God takes the righteous soul to a place called "*heichal ahava,*" a sanctuary where hidden treasures are kept for the righteous for the period after the Resurrection. In this special place, the pure love that

God has toward the righteous and vice versa, is likened to the parental love a father has toward a daughter, who by nature embraces her, kisses her and gives her presents. So too, God embraces these precious souls every day.

Midnight Highlights

Another highlight of lower Gan Eden takes place every night beginning at *chatzot*, midnight. This is the time of *ratzon*, free will, when God comes down to lower Gan Eden in order to delight the righteous souls therein. With the trees singing and praising God, a spirit from the north awakens and plays the harp of David. The angel Gavriel then announces loudly (so that the souls in heaven and on Earth hear), that there is now a special opportunity for those who have concentrated intent to absorb secrets and treasures that will be revealed from upper Gan Eden. All of the passageways of the gates of heaven and of Gan Eden and of the various temples are open in order to receive the prayers of individuals. Simultaneous to this, all of the mitzvot and acts of kindness performed by the soul in this world are raised to the heavens in an act of great unity of positively holy powers and divine illuminations (Zohar Lech Lecha, Folio 77; Zohar Vayikra, Folio 22).

Moving Further Upwards

It is possible that, after a while, the soul can undergo a process of moving up spiritually. Further purification does not take place in Gan Eden, but rather in *Nahar d'Nur* or through another gilgul. It depends upon the soul's desire. Hence, as stated above, before a soul is raised from lower to higher Gan Eden, it must again immerse itself in the River of Light so that it will forget and forsake the furor of emotions experienced in knowing God.

During the process of moving to upper Gan Eden, cloud and smoke envelop the soul in order to mask its entry so that others below do not witness it. Why? The Talmud (Bava Batra 75) explains that each man is "burned" by the canopy of his fellow man. This means that when we see something virtuous in someone else, we "prosecute" ourselves by saying, "what do I have to do in order to achieve that as well?" It is meant here in its positive sense of self-betterment. God is showing His mercy here by masking those going upwards because He knows that souls at this stage cannot do anything to better themselves (unless they do another gilgul). Only those souls who are worthy of this "promotion" hear themselves being called by a four-faced eagle.

Upon entering, God causes the horizon to rotate three times around Gan Eden so that the souls can see the pleasantness of this sight. They then bow down and enter through a circular pillar couched by cloud and smoke (Maavar Yabok, Siftei Renanot, Chapter 35).

The societies of upper Gan Eden are organized into *yeshivot* (schools) in which a higher understanding of the divine mind is attained. Each night at midnight, the Holy One appears and enters Gan Eden to share His blessed wisdom with the righteous that have merited entry into the upper Gan Eden.[19]

Rabbi Eliahu ben Shlomo Zalman (also known as The Gra or The Vilna Gaon) says that the newly arrived righteous receives 150 days during which to give his own public discourses on what he learned in the previous world (Even Shlayma 10:28).

If a soul reaches lower Gan Eden without knowledge, he will have to reincarnate in order to learn the basics of life, because in lower Gan Eden souls gain additional knowledge. Gaining the basics is a prerequisite to understanding the lessons to be learned in lower Gan Eden. Gaining entrance to upper Gan Eden heavily depends upon one's thoughts, intent and the intensity with which one performed mitzvot (Zohar Chadash, Vol. III, Folio 86b).

An example of this type of intensity is a story told of Rabbi Perachia who spent all of his money in order to perform the mitzvah of burying the dead. The person who was buried by him received permission to immediately come back to this world to show Rabbi Perachia parts of Gan Eden.[20]

For the first 12 months after transitioning, the body still has influence over its neshama as it continues on its journey. Even though the soul reaches the lower Gan Eden, it goes down to its previous mental state whilst in its body. After 12 months, however, the soul wears its spiritual gown and is anointed in the world of souls. Lower Gan Eden is not the final place where the soul reaps the fruits of its merits. This realm serves to act as an entrée to the next step—to upper Gan Eden (Shaar Hagmul, p. 356). Rabbi Azulai adds that in the lower Gan Eden God heals wounds sustained during the gehinom process.

From all of the descriptions above, it is easier to understand how a soul could want to tear itself away from this bliss in order to get to the next level of honor. Souls are exposed to so many righteous souls that they may wish to undergo another gilgul in order to personally experience something different/better for themselves and thereby move up another notch spiritually. Should they decide to do so, the following eight steps (34–41) are taken in preparation for rebirth.

Step 34: Space of Protection

Even though souls may be overwhelmed by the wonderful surroundings in lower Gan Eden and have a genuine sense of accomplishment at reaching this stage, they are expected to practice and devote time to mentally concentrate on assisting people on Earth, especially relatives and friends. If we become angry, resentful, and confused by our life situations, this does not necessarily mean we possess an underdeveloped spirit. Soul development is a complex matter where we all progress by degrees in an uneven manner. The important thing is to recognize our faults, avoid self-denial, and have the courage and self-sufficiency to make constant adjustments in our lives. People tend to think of souls as being without deficiencies and this isn't so. Souls work on special energy projects on their own. In order to do this, they go to a place Newton calls the "place of protection." Here they enter an interdimensional field of floating, silvery-blue energy and project outward to geographical areas of their choosing. Souls ride on their thought waves to specific people, buildings, or a given area of land in an attempt to comfort or effect change.

Step 35: Space of Transformation

The "soul searching" that *neshamot* do is hard work. After the strenuous mental efforts from the previous step, some souls choose to go into solitude and some go to Earth for relaxation and recreation. Right after a hard life, a soul can also go into solitude for a lengthy period of adjustment alone. The vacations on Earth are to re-experience former physical environments.

The Space of Transformation is where souls are able to study and practice many arts. Souls use this space for the sheer enjoyment of reshaping and enhancing their inherent energy sources. Playful competition exists but without the emotional aggression one sees in sports on Earth. Guides encourage game participation as a means of practicing energy movement, dexterity, and group thought transmission. Examples of games played: tag, red rover, dodgeball (large numbers of souls line up opposite each other and throw bolts of energy. They can be dodged or caught and thrown back. The object is not to be inadvertently hit by a bolt). Gemball, a game combining marbles and lawn bowling, gives one the means to learn about the personal aspects of one's soul. A soul might make a decision to be with certain people based on this game (Newton, *Destiny of Souls*, pp. 309–310).

The evening hours are specially designated for recreation time for the *nefesh*, and midnight for the *ruach* (Chesed L'Avraham 5:41, pp. 227–228). Each of those respective hours are more conducive to their particular spiritual development.

While leisure times are for rejuvenation and entertainment, there are soul-group counterparts who choose to further their learning instead.

Step 36: Ring of Destiny/Life Selection

Thus far we have seen that God opens up many different kinds of rooms to a soul in the afterlife. Some of these rooms can be understood as existing in the literal sense and some in the ethereal sense. Since souls have the ability to travel to a place via their thoughts, we can appreciate the wide range of options available to it.

The Ring of Destiny room is filled with a high concentration of force fields with glowing energy screens. It has been described by

Newton's patients as a circular domed theatre with floor-to-ceiling panoramic screens surrounding the soul completely. The Ring displays futuristic scenes of events ("post life progression") and the people to be encountered in the life to come. It also displays past life review scenes. It is designed to give the soul an ability to either observe or participate in the action, just as in the libraries. Scenes are also edited for their benefit. Some souls are shown certain years in great detail while other parts of their future life are completely left out.

Souls take a portion of their energy, leaving the rest at the console and can enter the 3-D illuminated viewing screens in one of two ways: as observers moving as unseen spirits through scenes on Earth with no influence on events, or as participants where they assume roles in the action of the scene even to the extent of altering reality from the original. Because this is only a re-creation, it doesn't influence others around the soul—just the soul itself for learning purposes. One client said that, "these records give the illusion of books with pages, but they are sheets of energy which vibrate and form live picture-patterns of events" (Newton, *Destiny of Souls*, pp. 162–163). Legendary baseball player Yogi Berra was once quoted as saying: "Prediction is a very difficult art—especially when it involves the future." For many, observing certain aspects of their future gives them confidence. It is like doing a full dress rehearsal before the actual performance (of a new life). We see some alternative routes to the main road, although the routes are not fully exposed.

It is noteworthy to mention here that on Earth God hides many of the sights and events that surround us daily. We see the past and the present only. This allows us to focus on what we have to do today without the distraction of what will be. In the next world, however, it will be possible to view the past, present and future all at once. Rabbi Chaim Friedlander, in his book *Siftei Chaim*, explains that the concept of "eternity" *(netzach)* is above time, and therefore is not limited by the dimensions of the past, present and future. His master teacher, HaRav Eliezer Dessler, further elucidates this point by giving the following example. Imagine a map covered over by a sheet of paper with a small window cut out in the paper. When the window sits on top of a name of a city, we see it—that represents the present. If the window is moved to another city, the previous one that was visible is now covered again, representing the past. The ones not uncovered as yet represent the future. In the next world, this map "cover" will be removed from us and hence it will be possible to see the past, present, and future all at once. In effect, they all become one in the present.

Step 37: Choosing a New Body

There are a number of angel specialists who work together with souls in this room. Archivist Souls assist in searching out past histories and alternative timelines to those events. Time masters track timelines of the immediate future for bodies under consideration. Planners choose bodies for souls that are intended to combine specific personality combinations. When a soul joins with a new baby, the partnership will address both the soul's shortcomings and a body-mind who needs this particular soul (Newton, *Destiny of Souls*, pp. 365, 388).

"Accountability for wrongdoing frequently comes with the selection of the next body for the payment of karmic debts. Souls are directly involved with this selection process through their Council because this is what they want for themselves. Although karma is associated with justice, its essence is not punitive but one of bringing balance to the sum of our deeds in all past lives." (ibid., p. 252)

Just as the soul is "weighed in" on the scale of deeds upon its arrival, here too souls are weighed in order to clarify their level of suitability to the body they will enter (Zohar Mishpatim, Folio 95b).

If souls choose a life where their death will be premature, they often see it in the Place of Life Selection (previous step). These souls essentially volunteer in advance for bodies that will have sudden fatal illnesses, are to be killed by someone, or come to an abrupt ending from a catastrophic event. These souls do not happen to be in the wrong place at the wrong time with God looking the other way. Every soul has a motive for the events in which it chooses to participate. One Newton client said that he chose to enter the body of a Native American boy who would die at age seven because "I was looking for a short burst lesson in humility" and this life as a mistreated starving child was enough.

Living in a handicapped body does not necessarily mean one is paying a karmic debt. When a soul is inside a damaged body, it is there in order to learn some kind of lesson. The Chofetz Chaim, an influential Eastern European rabbi of the nineteenth century once said that these souls are totally pure and they come to this world in an otherwise limited body in order to be an object of love for someone else. By doing so, they promote acts of kindness on the part of others.

Likewise, each of us voluntarily agrees to be the child of a given set of parents (Newton, *Journey of Souls*, p. 247). If hurtfulness instead of love abounds, we are not the victims of biological parents whom we inherited, rather a karmic purpose is at work here. It is important to remember that we come to Earth to play a part in the drama of others' lessons as well. We don't need to change who we are in relation to life's experiences, we only need to control our negative reactions to these events (Newton, *Destiny of Souls*, p. 351).

While choosing a new body, souls preview the life span of more than one human being in the same time cycle. When leaving this area, most souls are inclined toward one particular body for soul occupation. However, our spiritual advisors give us ample opportunity to reflect upon all we have seen in the future before making a final decision.

The Zohar (Pt. II, fol. 96b; III, 388) states that when the time arrives for embodiment,each soul is called before the Holy One and is told which physical body to inhabit. This, at first, seems to contradict what we've described above, that the soul indeed has a choice of which body to enter next. The exception to the rule is first-time souls, who are told by God which body they will enter; in subsequent incarnations, the choice is left up to the soul. Rabbi Yitzchak Danzig of Peterborg once said that souls, upon descending from the next world back to this world, have a difficult time withstanding the foul odor of Earth. Therefore, in order to make a smooth initial transition, souls take with them blades of grass from Gan Eden, whose pleasant aroma chases away the foul odor (Stories from *The World of Truth*, p. 240).

Furthermore Rav Shimon stated that Adam was shown impending generations—not spiritually, but actually (Zohar Lech Lecha 90b). When the neshamot were created in otzar haneshamot, they all stood in front of God in the form and image that they will take when coming down to this world. When a person dies, he sheds the physical body, but he receives an image that is very similar to that of how he looked in this world (same face and body image). In lower Gan Eden we get a new set of clothing that we are happier with— the very same ones we wore up in otzar haneshamot before coming down to Earth for the first time. That is why NDErs are so willing to remain in the dimension they reached on their brief visit in the afterlife. In their journey they are freed of their physical body, but retain a spiritual image and facial likeness.

When a soul enters this world, it dresses itself with the clothing of tzelem (spiritual image, semblance, form) whose source represents a combination of good and evil. In the case of a first-time soul for example, if the father and mother were having inappropriate thoughts while having marital relations, this causes the evil inclination to have a stronger influence on the child and affect the preconceived plans of the soul while in the Ring of Destiny. It must then compensate for any additional bumps along the way. These additional bumps are the will of God and thus the soul will come down to this world against its own wishes.

As we've explained in Step 24 (Transition) the Zohar teaches that upon a soul's departure from this world and again upon entering this world, it is placed on a scale to be "weighed in." Its merits are weighed in order to determine its spiritual place in the next world. Likewise its readiness and maturation are weighed at this stage to clarify which type of body it merits on its upcoming journey to Earth.

Step 38: Prompters

Prompters are special guides/speakers who come up with ingenious ideas so we will know what to look for in our next life. Signs are placed in our minds at this stage in order to jog our memories later on as humans—like markers in the road of life. People we will meet in our next life are presented now so that we'll recognize them later. These triggers are supposed to click in our memory right away and tell us "oh good, you're here now." These flags are designed to point us in the right direction whenever we find ourselves at a crossroad.

In Tractate *Nidah—Perek Hamapelet*, the Talmud mentions that the Torah we were taught in utero is forgotten in order to re-learn it through much effort and hard work. Plato echoes this thought, saying that in order for man to understand, he needs to be reminded of that which he was already exposed to as a soul.

Step 39: Preparation for the Descent

Souls attend a "recognition class"—pretty much like cramming for a final exam. It is an aspect of spiritual reinforcement that occurs just before embarking on the passage back to Earth. The Zohar tells us that when a soul is in the act of descending towards this world, it visits that part of lower Gan Eden where "souls of the just" (righteous) gather after they have left this life (Tazria, Folio 43). It also goes to *Sheol* and sees the souls of the wicked.

The spirit of the neshama travels from olam habriya to lower Gan Eden via a place between olam hayetzira and olam haasiya (where the spirits in upper Gan Eden reside). In this in-between place, the neshama is delayed or held until it is ready to stand up to the challenges of entering a physical body—the soul has to fill out and thicken a bit. It also derives strength from the light of the four spiritual winds corresponding to the earthly physical winds—namely fire, wind, water, and dust (Zohar Shemot, Folio 13). Likewise, all souls receive certain powers from God before they come down to this world (Zohar Beshalach, Folio 54). This is the same place that neshamot rest until it is time for them to reincarnate (Zohar Vayechi, Folio 228b). This location is different, though, from the "holding place" mentioned earlier in Step 17. In order to visualize this, imagine the following locations layered around one another beginning with an inner core and then subsequent outer rings around it (see Figure 2).

The form of the neshama is similar to the form of its body—just thinner. Before it descends it dresses up with its tzelem and removes its spiritual clothing of Gan Eden. This clothing is hidden away until its return to Gan Eden. As already discussed, God causes it to forget its past and future appearances in Gan Eden in order to preserve free choice—otherwise it will not eat, drink or build (Zohar Terumah, Folio 150).

A nice summary of souls getting ready for its descent to this world is provided by the Zohar Chadash in Parshat Acharei Moat, Vol. II, Folio 57b, as follows:

Two angels, the *yetzer tov* (good inclination) and *yetzer rah* (evil inclination) tell the soul that God commanded that they must leave the temple of souls and depart to this world, enter a physical body, and then occupy itself with the performance of good deeds. This soul is shown all of Gan Eden so it will know the reward it will receive if it performs mitzvot. The soul is also shown all of the glorious temples and dwellings and all of the various levels in lower Gan Eden. The soul then asks which part of all this will I merit? One of the answers is that he will inherit 42 temples of various glory and beauty if he reads the prayer for the *Shema* properly each day at the appropriate time.

The soul is then shown other temples. Afterwards he is led to gehinom escorted by a cloud during the day and by a special fire at night. It is dark and he is shown the various levels, the rotating sword, and vicious dogs that scare souls. He is also shown 42 temples and people whose hands and feet are tied up and shouting bitter regrets for not going to pray in a synagogue, having recited the Shema or having donned Tefillin.

BACK TO THE AFTERLIFE

It is pointed out that every soul comes to gehinom—even those of the righteous. However those who learn Torah and perform mitzvot receive a special angel who accompanies him when he reaches this point in order to protect him.

After all this, the yetzer tov makes the soul promise to follow the Torah's precepts. The yetzer rah then warns the soul that it will have to overcome the depravity of this world and its sinful challenges.

Upon birth into this world, the yetzer tov grabs the soul by its collar and causes it to forget all of the Torah the angel taught him in the womb, and makes a mark above his mouth, saying: "Do not forget the promise you made to me."

Step 40: Meeting with God Himself

At the precise hour a soul is to descend, God calls upon the minister in charge and tells him "bring me soul X." When the soul stands before God, God tells it what his role and purpose will be in the world it will soon be entering and makes it swear that it is committed to this. Likewise, Jewish souls promise they will recognize the Almighty and will try to learn the hidden treasures of the Torah while on Earth in order for the shechina to continue shining forth in this world as it does in the upper world (Zohar Terumah, Folio 161b). This shows that there are times when God wants to personally bond with the neshama without the intervention of angels.

Paralleling this meeting that Jewish souls have with the Almighty, many of Newton's patients reported meeting with a second Council of Elders, similar to the phase described in Step 27. The soul again appears in the presence of the Council as a final stage before rebirth. The Elders want to reinforce the significance of a soul's goals for the next life. The soul goes to a white space, which is like being in a cloud-filled enclosure. The atmosphere is formal, but calm and friendly. Each Elder in turn asks questions in a gentle way. They want the soul's input to assess motivations and the strength of its resolve towards working in a new body. They stress the benefits of persistence and holding on to values under adversity. They give the soul inspiration, hope and encouragement to trust himself in bad situations and not to let things get out of hand. And then as a final act to bolster confidence, they raise their arms and send a power bolt of positive energy into the soul's mind to take with him back to Earth.

Step 41: Farewell to Cluster Group

The soul either returns to its cluster group for a final goodbye or it directly proceeds to incarnate.

Step 42: Rebirth

The transition of souls from the spirit world to the mind of a baby is relatively more rapid than the passage back to the afterlife. The reason for this is that a soul coming to the spirit world from Earth needs more time to acclimate. Coming from the all-knowing state of the spirit world, souls are mentally able to adjust more quickly to the new surroundings.

While in the womb, a soul can stray from the uterus when it is bored. A baby's mind must be ready to connect with the soul, but until it is born, the soul is free to join other similar souls. They usually like to revisit places where they lived together in former lives.

Step 43: Return to Lower Gan Eden

After completing a gilgul, the soul returns to its elevated place in lower Gan Eden and can now either feel content to stay at this spiritual level or proceed upward.

Many returning souls skip steps on the map because they are more familiar with the routine. So, for example, less time may be spent with the Guide, no orientation may be necessary, and time in *gehinom* could be curtailed. I do believe that returning souls still follow the general path outlined in the steps delineated up to now but at varying levels of intensity depending on the spiritual attainment achieved in the most immediate past life.

Step 44: Moving Up the Rung of The Seven Heavens

When God created the world, he formed seven heavens (*rikiim*) below it and seven above it. The seven heavens above the world, according to The Vilna Gaon, are located between the lower and upper Gan Eden (Even Shlayma 10:15). Each heaven above has its own solar system and stars, and different kinds of angels (four- or six-winged, two or four-faced, or one-faced). Some have the appearance of fire, water or wind. The heavens are positioned directly on top of each other, closely clad like "the skins on an onion" (Reisheet Chochma, Shaar Ahava 5:28). In order to move up these rungs, the soul must give a further accounting of his character at each heavenly stage.

45. Upper Gan Eden

As opposed to lower Gan Eden, which is situated on the Earth's plane, upper Gan Eden is located in olam habriya on the horizon. There are three walls surrounding upper Gan Eden. This place can be reached by those righteous individuals who have mastered their thoughts (ibid., Shaar Kedusha 4:21). For example, we derive bodily pleasure in this world from eating and drinking in the form of how it looks, tastes, smells, feels, and perhaps from feeling satiated. Elevating this worldly action a notch, the righteous eat and drink for the higher purpose of maintaining physical health in order to better serve God. The righteous are steeped in the thought of eating at the table of God in the next world.

Each righteous person has his own paradise carved out specifically for him to bask in the pleasures of the Divine light. Souls who merit entering can do so only on the Sabbath or other holidays. All of the beauty described in lower Gan Eden exists here as well (Tractate Seder Gan Eden). For example, it is a place that is well stocked with the best the land can offer. Many persimmon rivers flow alongside fruit-bearing trees and wondrous sweet plantations (Nishmat Chaim Article 1:10). The angel Michael precedes the newly admitted souls of the righteous and introduces them as they arrive in upper Gan Eden (Zohar Chaye Sara, Folio 125b).

Seven names were given to upper Gan Eden: *tsror hachayyim* (eternal life), *ohel Hashem* (God's tent), *har hakodesh* (holy mountain), *har Hashem* (God's mountain), *mekom hakodesh* (the holy place), *chatzrot Hashem* (God's courtyard), and *beit Hashem* (house of God). In the Zohar (Vayakhel) it says that there exists a pillar[21] that connects lower Gan Eden to upper Gan Eden and it is called *"machon har tzion"* (the dwelling place of Mount Zion).

Even after a righteous soul enters upper Gan Eden, it comes down to lower Gan Eden to visit. Just like the soul goes up and down from lower Gan Eden to Earth during the first 12 months after transitioning (because it has a hard time separating from its body), so too the soul visits and appreciates the blissful place of lower Gan Eden, which served as a stepping stone to enter upper Gan Eden. The soul remains in lower Gan Eden in the Heichal appropriate for it until it learns and gets wiser (Zohar Breisheet, Folio 38b). During the time it is mourning over its body, it stays in lower Gan Eden. There are souls who are ready to move on after a month and others only after 12 months. The soul then travels through different heichalot which include trees, flowers, roses, grass and fruit, all indicating what awaits in upper Gan Eden where the soul will understand the hidden treasures of Hashem and His greatness (ibid., Folio 41).

Other reasons for coming down to lower Gan Eden include having the opportunity to greet newcomers with enthusiasm, especially relatives or others beloved to them while on Earth. They go so far as to ask them for updates on what has been happening on Earth (Nishmat Chaim, Article 1:10).

Let's now briefly review where each part of the soul goes upon death. The neshama goes to upper Gan Eden, the ruach to lower Gan Eden, and the nefesh stays with the body in the grave in order to protect it from destroyers. The impurities stick to the body and flesh and not to the bones so that the nefesh can watch over the bones until the Resurrection. On Shabbat and holidays, the neshama, which resides in upper Gan Eden, communicates with the ruach in lower Gan Eden and then returns to upper Gan Eden. After Shabbat when the ruach returns to its place in lower Gan Eden, it brings with it a big light that it received from above and from this light it illuminates the nefesh in the kever and dresses in the tzelem, or image, of the body. With this levush (clothing), the bones rise up from the kever on Saturday nights and sing praises to God.

If we were able to see upper images, on Saturday nights, on the eves of rosh chodesh, and on holidays we would witness them standing upon their graves and praising God.[22] (Zohar Terumah, Folio 142).

Step 46: *Techiyat Hameitim* (Resurrection)/ *Olam habba* (World to Come)

The Ultimate Destination

"In the sixth century of the sixth millennium, the gates of the supernal wisdom will be opened, as will the springs of the earthly wisdom, preparing the world to be elevated in the seventh millennium" (Zohar Vayera, Folio 117).

In the seventh millennium both the moon and the sun will shine seven times as bright as they do in this world (Isaiah 30:26). They will both also dry up, signifying the destruction of mankind and the physical world as we know it. After the Resurrection, the world (in the eighth millenium) will arise anew and mankind will be rejuvenated and live forever, as will the sun and the moon (Shaar Hagmul, p. 394).

Rabbinic afterlife teachings varied in different places and times, and were never synthesized into one coherent philosophy. As such, the different descriptions of the afterlife are not always consistent with each other. This is especially true for the descriptions of olam habba, the World to Come. In some rabbinic works this phrase refers to the messianic era, a physical realm right here on Earth. However, in other works this phrase means Gan Eden, a purely spiritual realm. The future world (after the Resurrection) will be built with total kindness—klipot, the evil inclination, and death will all be abolished, allowing one to derive pleasure from the splendor of the light of the righteous. Furthermore, there shall be no limitation to the moon's light and no judgment—the honor of God will be within reach of all with other unlimited benefits.

It's a matter of debate in Jewish tradition as to whether the post-Resurrection life is permanent, or temporary. Nachmanides believes that the ultimate reward, the "World to Come," is post-Resurrection life, and therefore it must be eternal. Maimonides (The Rambam), on the other hand, holds that the ultimate reward is the relatively direct experience of God that a soul can have when not encumbered with a body and its desires. Therefore he understands the phrase "World to Come" to refer to the non-physical existence after life that is man's ultimate reward.

Rabbi Yosef Albo, a Jewish philosopher who lived in Spain during the fifteenth century and known chiefly as the author of *Sefer Ha-Ikkarim* ("Book of Principles"), the classic work on the fundamentals of Judaism, agrees with Maimonides that the post-Resurrection life isn't permanent. Specifically, he believes that the lifespan will be 1,000 years—the length of time Adam would have lived after eating from the forbidden fruit had he not given away 70 years to King David.[23] Albo writes that in this life, man masters the art of self-perfection in the face of adversity—disease, threat of poverty, and everything else that could go wrong in life. In the next life, the only challenges are internal. It is therefore a second step in personal development, allowing for more refinement in one's ability to enjoy the World to Come upon return.

The Rambam maintains that the World to Come is the World of Souls (*Olam Haneshamot*), which is often referred to as Gan Eden.

Ultimately, when the time comes for the Resurrection, this will be (as conceived by the Rambam) a transient stage, for after the Resurrection, the body will again die, and only the soul will return to the World to Come, i.e., to the World of Souls.

In contrast to the view of the Rambam, most other authorities hold that the phrase "World to Come" in the Talmud refers to the era of the Resurrection of the Dead.

In other words, the Rambam believes that after the Resurrection of the Dead, people will still die and inherit their ultimate reward in the World of Souls. Other authorities maintain that after death, all souls abide in the World of Souls until the Resurrection, at which time they are finally enclothed in a body in olam habba.

It should be noted that this difference of opinion between the Rambam and the other authorities was meaningful only in their days. Since then Rabbi Yitzchak Luria—whose pronouncements in the esoteric areas of the Torah have been universally accepted—ruled according to the majority opinion (as stated in above paragraph "the other authorities maintain...") and hence this has been universally accepted.[24]

Closing Thought

As we have just witnessed from the long 46 step virtual tour of the afterlife, there is indeed much that is positive to look forward to. We are not cognizant that all of this exists because we are too focused on facing the challenges we are given here on Earth. We are too preoccupied with earning a living, and when we find the job that defines us, we toil too many hours in performing it. We have reduced ourselves to scraping by on a paycheck in order to survive another week instead of working in order to live.

Many of the great Rabbis of the Talmudic era and thereafter

worked the minimum number of hours a day in order to support their families. The rest of the day and night was spent in Torah study —the major purpose and focus in their lives. Today, while there are indeed many dedicated individuals who sit and learn Torah as their primary occupation, the majority of us are caught in a vicious cycle of waking up early, going to sleep late, answering to an unsympathetic boss, paying endless bills, worrying about finances, paying high tuition, and annually forcing ourselves to take a vacation that is forgotten all too soon thereafter. If we could only be bold enough to take the knowledge and awareness of these 46 steps and apply the perspective we have gained from them to every breathing moment we have in this world, we would be on course to living our current lives in a much wiser, more productive and compassionate fashion. Imagine yourself traveling forward in time, getting a healthy dose of perspective, and then returning to the present with a revitalized sense of purpose and commitment. One of my objectives in life has been to bring this awareness to you. There is no day like today to seize the moment.

CHAPTER FIVE

Olam Habba: The Order of Things in the World to Come

"I believe that when people die, they go to the same place as all the people who haven't yet been born. That's why it's called the world to come, because that's where they make the new souls for the future. And the reward when good people die... is that they get to help make the people in their families who haven't been born yet..."

—Dara Horn

ANY OF US have a tendency to utilize the term *olam hab-ba* (the world to come) in a loose, general way. What we are basically referring to is the "next" world, the world that awaits us once the promise of Resurrection is fulfilled by God. But what does this future reality comprise? And when does it occur?

The afterlife essentially has two parts—the time before the Resurrection and after. Before the Resurrection, we will exist only in soul form, in Gan Eden, whereas after the Resurrection, we will exist in both body and soul, pretty much as we now exist in this world.

Up to this point, we've become aware of the following landmarks in our souls' journey:

- This World
- Death
- World of Souls (Olam HaNeshamot—Gan Eden)
- Days of Messiah
- Day of Judgment and Resurrection—(Where both the soul and body receive reward)
- Olam Habba—(Where the body further purifies itself and approaches the level of spirituality of its nefesh counterpart)

The righteous are said to be "invited" to olam habba, the world that we inhabit once the Resurrection occurs. But before the Resurrection of body and soul, the Messiah must arrive to usher in this new era.

Days of the *Mashiach* (Messiah)

The Days of the Mashiach are associated with the sixth millennium (Zohar Vayera, Folio 119), during which two redeemers will usher in the Messianic era. Mashiach ben Yosef will act as a precursor to Mashiach ben David, the final redeemer, and will prepare the world for him by initiating the ingathering of the exiles. The Zohar states that in the year 5060 Mashiach ben Yosef will appear and 13 years later Mashiach ben David (some say this is the year 5673 corresponding to the year 1913, the year before World War I began), whereupon the nations of the world will conspire against Israel (some other sources say this was to be the year 5661 or 5600). Over the following 27 years world wars will continue; however, the kingdoms of the nations who come to Jerusalem soil to capture it will be eliminated in the outskirts of Jerusalem.

In another Zoharic source it states that the coming of the Messiah is slated to be in the 60th year after the millennia 6,000 (Zohar Chadash, Vol II, Folio 69b).

All of the various dates mentioned above are dates that have the potential to bring the final Redemption. We are told that the final redemption will arrive by the year 6,000—after that point we're in the World to Come. As we learn in Tractate Sanhedrin 97b, all of these dates have come and gone. The potential for the Mashiach to have come then depended not only on the arrival of the date itself, but also on the readiness of the Jewish People. That is to say, had the Jewish People repented and performed acts of chesed, the potential existed for the Mashiach to have arrived. It is up to the Jewish people as a nation to strive toward this goal so that the Mashiach could come sooner than the year 6000. The Talmud goes on to say that if not, then by that year he will surely come even without our repentance. Under those circumstances, he will come with a cost that will be higher in terms of quality of life, and even at the cost of life itself for many.

The Zohar in Shemot (Folios 7-9) also describes how the *Mashiach* will be revealed. While this topic is beyond the scope of this book, I will just mention here that the Mashiach will be a righteous man born naturally to parents (as opposed to the notion that he will magically appear in some supernatural way), and that he will only know that he is indeed Mashiach when an additional neshama enters his own neshama thereby awakening his cognizance of who he is and what his mission is to be. This additional neshama will provide the support and determination he needs to carry out his task.

Day of Judgment and Resurrection

Rabbi Yosai teaches (Zohar Chaye Sara, Folio 124) that when the time gets close to the Resurrection, God will make an announcement to the Israelites to "sing to God a new song" (*Shiru L'Hashem shir chadash*). Since death will be abolished after the Resurrection, continues Rabbi Yosai, it is fitting during the time of the Mashiach to sing this new song as the imminent new world is about to unfold. Furthermore, whoever sings the psalm *"az yashir"* everyday will merit chanting it in olam habba (Zohar Beshalach, Folio 54b).

However, there is a caveat to this scenario. The Talmud tells us that the world will exist for 6,000 years, but if the Mashiach does not come in that period of time, God will destroy the world in the seventh millennium after which He will rebuild it. During the seventh millennium God will create wings for the righteous so that they can fly upon the waters, as it is written: "Those who hope in the Lord will renew their strength. They will soar on wings like eagles; they will run and not grow weary..." (Isaiah 40:31).[1]

Rabbi Moshe Chaim Luzzato likened the entire period of time in this world until the days of the Mashiach to the period of life until the age of twenty (*Daat Tevunot*, p. 145). Until humans reach the age of twenty, life is like a training ground during which we engage in activities designed to educate and better ourselves. From age 20 onward, we will have gained the necessary tools to propel ourselves forward toward greater achievement. Thus, during the days of the Mashiach, there is the possibility to rise in the world of merits by leaps and bounds and it will be commonplace to witness people of very high esteem and intelligence.

Who Rises First?

There is a marked difference between the resurrections of bodies in Israel versus those outside of Israel. Bodies from abroad will rise but with a limited life-force. They will have enough energy to get up and travel under the Earth until they reach Israel, where they will be given their souls. Even the wicked will merit getting a spark of their soul at this time. Those bodies buried in Israel will rise first, being given their full life-force. The bodies all stand before God resembling their appearance when they lived in this world. God will then make an announcement at each grave and simultaneously the corresponding soul will descend from Gan Eden as a guiding light and shall illuminate the specific body to awaken and rise from the Earth, whereupon the world will be complete (Zohar Chaye Sara, Folio 131; Zohar Chadash, Vol. I, Folio 20b).

The specific place designated for the Resurrection to begin is Aram Naharayim, the region where Rachel was born. When the Temple was destroyed, she raised her voice and shed tears that flowed like a river, as it is written (Lamentations 2:18) "Let tears run down like a river..." [The reference here is to special dew that will come down and revive the dead (Zohar Vayeshev, Folio 182).]

The actual process of being resurrected is also well documented in Jewish text.[2] Interestingly, the soul actually worries that the physical body within which it resided will be allowed to rise at the Resurrection (Zohar Chaye Sara, Folio 123b). As already noted in the previous chapter (Step 6), the soul receives a pinkas that serves as authorization to enter lower Gan Eden. With this in hand, the soul makes a plea to the angel Dumah on behalf of its body. Dumah in turn gives a note to the angel Metatron in the graveyard listing those who merit rising (Metatron is the minister in charge of each soul's day to day affairs). The angel Gavriel is the one who actually puts a sign (the Hebrew letter Taf) on the foreheads of those who are to rise. Then Metatron comes to fix and prepare the bodies in order to receive their souls again. He also receives a note with the names of the righteous and which soul belongs to which body. Metatron actually builds the body anew from the luz, a small remaining bone in the grave that never decomposes (Zohar Chaye Sara, Folio 126b, 127b).

Beit Shammai, a Judaic school of thought founded by Shammai, a Jewish scholar of the first century says that when a fetus is created, the first part of it to be formed is the skin, then the muscles, then the veins and bones, and in the Resurrection first the bones will be formed, then the veins and muscles, and the skin last. Beit Hillel, a Judaic school lead by Hillel, the greatest sage of the second Temple period, however, says that the skin will be the first to be formed at the time of Resurrection. Most maintain that Beit Hillel is correct because in Ezekiel's resurrection of the dry bones is used as a metaphor for the renewal of the people of Israel and in this particular story, God performed an unusual miracle to show the Jewish nation that they could believe that there in fact will be (a spiritual resurrection now and) a physical resurrection in the world to come (Zohar Pinchas, Folio 222). God promises to burn all the wickedness from the world, cancel death forever (Zohar Bereisheet, Folio 29), and uproot all of the chariots of the evil inclination (Zohar Beshalach, Folio 51b). He will call each soul by his name and everyone will rise in the same manner as one rises out of bed, apart from those that did not repent. They will be like dust under the legs of the righteous. In such a case, when a man does not merit existing in his own right, he still can be of service to others, even as an inanimate object (Tikunei HaZohar, Folio 81).

At the time of the Resurrection, souls will also achieve a higher level of perfection. When Adam sinned, all souls were damaged to a degree, but after the Resurrection, Jews will perform their worship in perfection because the impurities caused by the temptation of the snake will have disintegrated, and whatever is crooked within the soul will be straightened out and fixed. While the majority of commentators believe this process will involve reassembling the physical body previously inhabited, a minority opinion maintains that it involves the materialization of the spiritual body. Those souls that have not completed their spiritual body to perfection will, at the Resurrection, materialize here on Earth in order to perform the remaining *mitzvot* required of them in an environment free of death and evil.

The Talmud relates that Rabbi Yehuda HaNasi, the compiler of the *Mishnah,* used to return in a spiritual body every Sabbath eve to sanctify the Sabbath by celebrating the *Kiddush* (sanctification over the wine) for his family. Having attained a fully spiritual body during his last incarnation on Earth, he was able to visit his family in this manner for an entire year. Only after one of the servants of the family revealed these visits to neighbors did Rabbi Yehuda HaNasi take final leave of his family, never to return again, on the grounds that his coming would put other saints to shame.

Yet even when a soul achieves the complete spiritual body, it is still not the ultimate state of being. Having attained such fullness, a soul can be "absorbed into the very Body of the King," the ultimate aim of its yearning and longing. Thus the soul merges finally in God, as a drop in the ocean (Rabbi Z. Schacter).

While in today's imperfect world the soul can only experience "reward" after it departs from the body, the soul and body will be reunited in the World to Come, and will together enjoy the fruits of their labor. As it is written in Isaiah, all those who died will be restored to life and their souls restored to their bodies; "Death will be eradicated forever" (Isaiah 25:8).[3]

Ten Things to Expect in Olam Habba

There are 10 things that God will bring forth anew in olam habba, following the Messiah's arrival (Shmot Rabba 15:21):

1 God will light up the world instead of the sun and the moon.
2 He will cause waters to spring forth from Jerusalem's Temple Mount (The Talmud, Tractate Shekalim 42), thus healing the sick.
3 He will cause the trees to bear new fruit every month and give them healing powers.
4 Mankind will build anew every place where there had been destruction.
5 He will build up Jerusalem with sapphire stone and the other nations of the world will recognize and respect the nation of Israel.
6 Cows and bears will graze together.
7 All of the animals will make peace with Israel and will not harm them.
8 Mankind will no longer cry and weep over troubles because there will be none.
9 Death will not exist anymore.
10 Mankind will have no reason to grieve or to worry.

Apart from the miraculous events listed above, other fascinating details have been documented about our existence in olam habba.

Eating and Drinking in Olam Habba

The Zohar describes a festive meal for the righteous in *olam habba* that consists of meat and fish, and wine preserved from the six days of Creation. This will take place after the Resurrection and its location will be in lower Gan Eden—somewhere between the physical and spiritual realm. Just as this plane is a cross between the physical and the spiritual, so too will our bodies be. Likewise, the food and drink referred to above will be the sum total of the average between physicality and spirituality. While some may take this literally, Rabbi Elazar believes that the soul is metaphorically feeding off of the splendor of the Shechina—the great light that nourishes one's soul (Zohar Toldot, Folio 135b). Rabbi Yehuda Srevnik adds that in the book Pri Tzaddik, HaRav Yitzchok M'Lublin comments that there are small divine sparks in every piece of food we eat here in this world that gives it vitality. This is even truer in olam habba when our food will be comprised of *"ziv hashechina,"* divine splendour, and there will be no need for physical consumption—it will be all spiritual. The Talmud (Brachot 17) adds that there will be no literal eating and drinking as the righteous will be sitting with crowns on their heads and taking pleasure in the countenance of the Divine light.

Dying for the Last Time

Why do some say it is necessary to die an additional time shortly after the Resurrection?

As stated earlier in this section, the Angel Dumah, who is the overseer of the dead, reports to the Angel Metatron, who is the overseer of the neshama. They speak about which bodies will resurrect and at what precise moment. Metatron's job is to take the *luz* from underneath this world and repair the dead bodies in order to prepare them for their revitalization at the time of the Resurrection, whereupon the body and soul will come together as one again. Due to the fact that *luz* comes from the material world and lasts 6,000 years, it is not spiritually ready to be alive in the seventh millennium, and therefore an additional bodily death is necessary after the Resurrection.

An example is given (Zohar Medrash HaNe'elam Vayera, 116) regarding the silversmith who submerges a silver coin into a burning fire until the earthly impurities are removed and what is left is just the silver. However, this silver is not entirely clean of all of its impurities. Hence, the silversmith places the silver into the flames again in order to remove the refuse. Similarly, God submerges a human body under the Earth and then rebuilds it from its dust after a second death. This second death lasts for a period of only three days.

According to the Ramchal, Rabbi Moshe Chaim Luzzato, the body feeds off of its soul in this world, but in the next world the soul will feed off of the body, which will be on a slightly higher level of purity than the soul. He explains this by saying that the ultimate Sabbath pleasure in the next world comes through the act of eating and drinking. This is backed up by Rabbi Menachem Schneerson (The Lubavitcher Rebbe), who said that the body does not know its real purpose in this world because it would disturb the natural order of free will and free choice. However, in the next world all of the existential reasons for being will become abundantly clear, hence we need to have two (types of) lives—one in this world and one in the next world. Similarly we grace the Sabbath by lighting two candles, blessing two *challot,* and ultimately basking in the coming of two Messiahs (Rabbi Moshe Armoni, *Resurrection and Secrets of the Soul,* CD).

Getting the Body into Shape

All physically challenged individuals who arrive in the next world will be healed. Moreover, whoever was obese in this world will be slim in the next world due to the "calories burned" while engaging in the draining efforts of Torah learning (*Sefer Hachezionot,* p. 237).

"Then will our Mouths be Filled with Laughter"

There is a verse in Tehillim (Psalms) 126:2 that is said to describe the Resurrection: "Then will our mouths be filled with laughter and our tongue with singing..."

To explain the verse, HaMagid HaYerushalmi, Rabbi Shabtai Yudelevitz, z"tl brought an example of a man dying at the young age of 20 and leaving behind a newborn baby. The fatherless child grows up to become an old man. When the hour of redemption and the Resurrection arrives, one can envision the old man walking over to the cemetery, making his way among the many thousands of people there who came to await the rise of their dear relatives. Lo and behold the old man beholds his father, risen from his grave looking exactly as he did when he died at the age of 20. The old man calls out with exuberance "father, father." All in earshot would certainly laugh at the strange sight—an old man walking alongside his 20-year-old father.

I believe that this last story sums up our lives in this world with an eye toward the afterworld. Most of us desire to live life to the fullest—to go out and have a good time in the present. We have at our disposal many forms of entertainment. But in Psalms 126:2, God reminds us that we shouldn't think that the world we live in now is the "be all and end all." If we live our lives as if there is no tomorrow, we may deprive ourselves of something better down the road. By anticipating that our mouths will be filled with laughter, we are reinforcing the notion that we shouldn't solely focus on the material rewards in this world, but look forward to an elevated version of our lives in the next world. By bringing death into the equation, God is instructing us to pause and absorb the fact that the purpose of our existence reaches far beyond what we see in this world. Happily, death is not the last stop on our journey.

I'd like to conclude this chapter with a highly inspirational story that essentially sums up what I have been emphasizing throughout this book:

There was a young woman who had been diagnosed with a terminal illness and had been given three months to live. So as she was getting her things "in order", she contacted her Pastor and had him come to her house to discuss certain aspects of her final wishes.

She told him which songs she wanted sung at the service, what scriptures she would like read, and what outfit she wanted to be buried in. Everything was in order and the Pastor was preparing to leave when the young woman suddenly remembered something very important to her.

"There's one more thing," she said excitedly.

"What's that?" came the Pastor's reply.

"This is very important," the young woman continued. "I want to be buried with a fork in my right hand." The Pastor stood looking at the young woman, not knowing quite what to say.

"That surprises you, doesn't it?" the young woman asked.

"Well, to be honest, I'm puzzled by the request," said the Pastor.

The young woman explained. "My grandmother once told me this story, and from that time on I have always tried to pass along its message to those I love and those who are in need of encouragement. In all my years of attending socials and dinners, I always remember that when the dishes of the main course were being cleared, someone would inevitably lean over and say, 'Keep your fork.' It was my favorite part because I knew that something better was coming... like velvety chocolate cake or deep-dish apple pie. Something wonderful, and with substance!

So, I just want people to see me there in that casket with a fork in my hand and I want them to wonder what's with the fork? Then I want you to tell them: "Keep your fork, the best is yet to come."

The Pastor's eyes welled up with tears of joy as he hugged the young woman good-bye. He knew this would be one of the last times he would see her before her death. But he also knew that the young woman had a better grasp of heaven than he did. She had a better grasp of what heaven would be like than many people twice her age, with twice as much experience and knowledge. She KNEW that something better was coming.

At the funeral people were walking by the young woman's casket and they saw the cloak she was wearing and the fork placed in her right hand. Over and over, the Pastor heard the question, "What's with the fork?" And over and over he smiled.

During his message, the Pastor told the people of the conversation he had with the young woman shortly before she died. He also told them about the fork and about what it symbolized to her. He told the people how he could not stop thinking about the fork and told them that they probably would not be able to stop thinking about it either.

So the next time you reach down for your fork, let it remind you, ever so gently, that the best is yet to come.

CHAPTER SIX

Connections Between This World and the Next

"This world is like a vestibule to the future world; prepare your-
self in the vestibule so you can enter the banquet hall."
—Ethics of the Fathers

T HE AVERAGE PERSON walking down the street may feel the
need to see something with their own eyes or hear something with their own ears in order to believe it. But there
are also millions who are perfectly willing to accept certain givens
on blind faith, such as solar systems that exist beyond the scope of
modern-day telescopes. In order to believe in something we cannot
see, we sometimes need to take a leap of faith.

Some say that for many years, the U.S. government has been
aware of UFOs and other paranormal phenomena, but keep quiet so
as not to distress the public or disturb the status quo.

A similar doubt encompasses the world of angels and spirits. Do
they really exist? What about dybbuks and ghosts? Is it possible for
the deceased to communicate with the living? Mediums will attest
to the existence of these spirits and their ability to pass along mes-

sages from another dimension. In light of what we have learned so far about the soul's journey, how can we make some sense out of these claims?

Paralleling the Afterlife

Everything in this life parallels the afterlife. All the joy we experience here is a taste of a far greater happiness to come. The bliss we experience from the natural beauty this world has to offer—the hill and the dale, the quiet spring of clear waters, the splendor of sunrise and sunset—are not deceptions. They stir within us immense love and yearning for the true beauty and genuine happiness of the afterlife, of which the soul possesses innate knowledge (Rabbi Avigdor Miller, *Sing You Righteous*).

Sleep reminds us of the inevitability of transitioning to the next world. Fire serves as a premonition of the great suffering that sin causes in gehinom. The Sabbath reminds us of the great state of happiness that occurs when the virtuous rest from the ordeals of life. Ants, known for their always busy-seeming manner, remind us of the necessity to prepare for eternity ("He who toils before the Shabbat, will eat on the Shabbat" (The Talmud, Avodah Zarah 3A)). When we awake in the morning from a night's sleep, the gratitude we are meant to have prepares us for the gratitude we will experience upon being resurrected. Thus as we walk through shopping centers and view the abundance of food and goods, and as we take delight from blossoming trees and gardens, we should accustom ourselves to blessing the Almighty as we will in the World to Come (Rashi commentary to The Talmud, Brachot 63A).

Influence of Earthly Acts on Souls in the Next World

If children do not follow in the evil ways of their parents, their deeds benefit their deceased parents' souls and affect their atonement. The Talmud (Moed Katan 28a) tells the story of a man who committed an indiscretion on Yom Kippur and was summoned to suffer in gehinom until the time his son was to be called up to the Torah to recite the blessings. The boy was born after the passing of his father, and out of residual anger toward the father, the community neglected to circumcise the boy. Rabbi Akiva, one of the greatest of the *Tannaim* (Scholars of the Mishnah), ordered the community to circumcise the boy and teach him the Torah and its blessings. He then summoned the community to call the boy up to the Torah on Shabbat. After this was done, the father appeared to Rabbi Akiva in a dream and told him that he had finally found peace of mind.

Because souls are incapable of acquiring new merit after death, the living can essentially transfer credit to the account of a loved one, thus enabling him to achieve higher status. One of the most potent methods of achieving this is by offering *tzedakah* (charity) in the name of the deceased. Another is learning Torah. Particularly potent in this regard is the study of *Mishnah* (the oldest authoritative collection of Jewish oral law), because it has the same Hebrew letters as the word *neshamah*, or soul.

Another way for the living to enable a discarnate soul to elevate spiritually is via the power of prayer, as illustrated by the following story. An elderly lady in a nursing home in the Midwest passed away. Her children, who always visited her and took care of her, dutifully performed a proper Jewish *tahara* (ritual purity) and burial.

On the fifth day of sitting shiva, the phone rang and the daughter sitting shiva answered the phone. On the other end of the phone was her mother. The daughter, in shock, immediately fainted. The phone rang again and it was her mother again, complaining that no one came to visit her that week. The family then rushed to the nursing home; it turned out there was a mixup and it was the mother's roommate who passed away and not, in fact, their mother. So now, the nursing home had the grim job of informing the children of the roommate that their mother had died five days earlier. The nursing home called and was trying to break it to these children slowly, but before they could even tell the children what happened, the children callously answered: "If this call has anything to do with our mother, we are not interested... All she does all day long is waste her time praying and saying Psalms." The children then added: "The one thing she prays for is that when she dies she should have a proper Jewish burial." "But," the children continued, "when she dies, we'll see to it that she doesn't get one." The nursing home staff then explained to them it was too late, as she already received her proper burial.[1]

Look at the power of prayer and to the extent God will go to in order to answer a prayer. In this case, He orchestrated a Divine confusion to respond to this woman's prayers. As a form of positive mental energy, prayer joins our energies with those of God, who seeks the growth and well-being of His children. Through prayer we cooperate with God and the angelic and spiritual beings of the spirit world in an ongoing cosmic effort to liberate humanity.

Because God looks to humankind as co-creators, and because He cherishes all efforts for the well-being of others, prayer is never wasted. Sooner or later, these efforts inevitably bear fruit, assisting in the positive advancement of those persons on whose behalf they are made. Calling out a specific name in prayer will draw cosmic energy to that person.

Our praying for someone who has passed on will give that soul "a boost" on the other side by enlisting the help of spiritual guides. Indeed, living in the spirit world, we may be even more sensitive to the beneficial effects of prayer than we were on Earth. Prayer ascends to gates that are commonly walled by numerous guardians, but those of the Palace of the Shechina have none, and prayers enter unhindered (Zohar Pt. II fol. 24a; I, 148).

Honoring one's parents is still in effect even if they are both deceased. Parents who are in lower Gan Eden are affected by the actions of their children who are still in this world. If they are not doing mitzvot, for example, the parents will not be able to enjoy their resting place (Zohar Yitro, Folio 93—Raya Mehemna). Parents may have done everything "right," but children could still go "off the path" due to the destiny of that neshama. Nonetheless, parents in lower Gan Eden can still feel grief over their children's ongoing behavior, as illustrated by the following dialogue between two friends. The thoughts in the following dialogue are primarily based on the Chafetz Chayim's (Rabbi Yisrael Meir Kagan) book, *Shmiras Haloshon:*

Menaseh: You mentioned yesterday that if a son goes on the wrong path it will be a great source of embarrassment for the father in the world to come. Can you elaborate on that?

Oded: The Zohar states that if a son goes on the wrong path he will certainly be disgracing his father. But if he goes on the right path it will be an honor for his father both in this world in the eyes of people and in the world to come before God.

Menaseh: How will he be honored before God?

Oded: The Zohar maintains that God will have mercy on the father as a result of his son and placed on a throne of honor.

Menaseh: Can you describe the embarrassment a father suffers if his son goes on the wrong path?

Oded: I will quote to you from the Vilna Gaon's famous letter, *Alim L'trufah*. He writes that even if one guides his son to the proper path but the son does not accept his guidance, woe is to the embarrassment, anguish and shame in the world to come. How much more so if the father causes his sons to turn from the proper path as a result of his approach, how much punishment, embarrassment and shame will come upon him. Each and every sin that his son commits will be a remembrance of sin for the father. Even when this son dies and the father is already sitting in Gan Eden he will still suffer. They will take him from his place in Gan Eden and bring him to gehinom to witness the suffering of his son.

Menaseh: That is very scary.

Oded: It certainly is. This should serve as a strong motivation for us to do everything in our power to assure that our children are getting a proper Torah education, one that will stay with them for the rest of their lives.

On the other end of the spectrum, there is a story told of a father's neshama who managed to get out of gehinom by virtue of the repentance done by his son in this world (Zohar Chadash, Vol. II, Folio 60b).

What solace can one bring to the children who still mourn over the absence of their beloved parent? The Zohar teaches us that the living can influence the status and well-being of the deceased (Zohar Chadash, Folio 60b) and the deceased can affect the well-being of those who are living (Zohar Shemot, Folio 16b). How so? Well, in the first case, when a soul goes up to Gan Eden, it is in a waiting mode until it reaches olam habbah after the Resurrection. While there, it is still able to decide to reincarnate to better itself or it can remain in Gan Eden and move up levels. One way it can move up levels is by continuing to derive nachat (comfort) from those offspring left behind in olam hazeh (this world).

If their offspring do chesed and mitzvot, then they derive pleasure and can enjoy their lot in Gan Eden. They can even be freed from a prolonged stay in gehinom due to the merits of their offspring here on Earth. If, on the other hand, their offspring conduct themselves in a manner that is offensive to Torah principles, then the parental soul that now resides in Gan Eden cannot enjoy its stay and can languish until some change is made. Similarly, when we say kaddish, we elevate the soul of our loved ones.

Soul Amnesia

Many of the customs of mourning have developed in order to assist the soul through its many trials in the afterlife. In order to help the soul overcome the amnesia it experiences when transitioning, it is customary for the mourners to remind the soul of its name. Reciting the mourner's kaddish helps "cool the fires of Gehenna." The maximum sentence for this purgatory is 12 months: however the mourner's kaddish recited for only 11 months so as not to insult the dead by assuming that he/she would have to serve the full term. The kaddish was not initially established for mourners. Kaddish was said at the end of a Torah class given by a rabbi and was designed to be a statement of faith that ultimately God's name should be and will be sanctified and magnified at a time when all the world will embrace the notion of a single God.

The spiritual power associated with the kaddish is considerable. R. Yehoshua ben Levi, a prominent rabbi in third-century Babylonia, declared, "(Even) a harsh sentence is torn up for anyone who replies *Amen Y'hei Shmei Rabbah M'vorach* (part of the Kaddish, which translates to: May His great name be blessed forever and to all eternity) with all their might." The Talmud and later midrashic (rabbinic interpretive) literature promote the concept that there are things that a child can do in this world to aid the parent who has passed on. At the moment he recites Barchu et Ado-nai Ham'vorach (the call to prayer, which literally means: Bless God, the blessed One), souls can be raised from the sentence of gehinom. We learn from here that a child has the power to elevate the soul of a parent in the afterlife.

Each year on a soul's *yahrzeit* (anniversary of death) it can reach a higher rung in Gan Eden. While the soul celebrates its birthday (of its return to heaven) with its celestial friends, the living celebrate the *aliyat ha-neshama* (ascendancy of the soul) by praying for a more exalted position in heaven for that soul.

Soul's Knowledge of This World

One may think that once a soul transitions to the next world, it knows the truth and is aware of all that goes on in this world. In truth, not all souls are aware of what goes on in this world—it depends upon how attuned they were to their surroundings when they were physically here (Zohar Omissions, Folio 303b). When someone dies, many souls are aware that the person is arriving and take on the responsibility of receiving the newcomer. In most cases, relatives are apprised so that they can welcome the soul. The main motivation of those in the higher realms is love, so there is great desire to help the new arrival leave the physical world in the best possible way.

Overhearing Souls Talking

A righteous man once gave a dinar (a coin of worth) to a poor man on the eve of the New Year. Being a year of drought, his wife became angry with him for giving away such a sum. He left the house and wandered over to the local cemetery to sleep. While there, he overheard two female souls talking about which crops will do well in the coming season. The man planted his field accordingly and subsequently earned a large sum of money (Tractate Brachot 18b).

On the eve of Hoshana Rabba (the seventh day of the Sukkot holiday), souls are believed to leave their graves in order to pray. In one tale, two people hid and heard one soul speaking to the next one about for whom they were going to pray and for what. These individuals subsequently told their community what they heard. On the eve of Hoshana Rabba the next year, two others hid in the cemetery in order to listen to the souls once again. This time they heard some of the souls saying that they would not gather together to pray because the community heard what they were saying last year, "therefore we will pray in our respective graves so that humans will not hear us."

It is also said that on Rosh Hashana (the Jewish New Year) the angel of death watches over those who were judged to death, and then lists their names in order to recognize them. But when God's mercy is elevated by the sound of the shofar, the angel of death gets confused to the point that he can no longer efficiently continue with his task until the holidays are over (Zohar Pekudei, Folio 238).

Deceased Harming or Helping the Living

"Let it not be said that the deceased cannot harm the living. A group of people once wanted to take a day trip. In a dream that night before, a deceased man came to one of the members of the group and said: 'Don't leave us because we get pleasure from your visiting the cemetery. If you leave us, be warned that you will be killed.' The group did not pay heed to the warning and they were subsequently all killed" (*Sefer Chasidim*, p. 218).

This story would be an extreme case of the dead influencing events on earth. However, the dead can also use their influence to protect the living. Caleb ben Yefuneh (a biblical character noted for his faith in God) bowed over the grave of his forefathers and asked them to pray to God that he be saved from the bad counsel of his peers. Knowing that the dead are aware of the suffering of the living, he recognized the benefit of praying at their graves. Caleb was saved as a result of his forefathers' prayer (Zohar Shemot, Folio 16b).

Another example refers to those who wake up at midnight in order to learn Torah. One is instructed to mouth the words of the Torah learning in an audible way, because the righteous in Gan Eden are listening. In the morning God extends to him His hand of chesed (Zohar Beshalach, Folio 46). The deceased can also present themselves before God and make a case to help their offspring. They can ask for permission to come down to this world in the form of a physical body and assist a loved one in need. There are other examples too. In a game played in San Francisco on August 22, 2007, The Chicago Cubs baseball team may have received supernatural intervention. Cliff Floyd, playing in his first game since taking a bereavement hiatus, hit a tiebreaking two-run single in a five-run ninth inning to lift the Cubs to a 5–1 victory over the San Francisco

Giants. Floyd said he felt the presence of his father, Cornelius, who passed away August 12. Floyd had spent the time away with his family and had not hit except for taking some swings in the batting cage the day before. "In my last at-bat, I said, 'You know, Pops... C'mon, let's do something,'" Floyd said. "It was definitely a weird feeling. I can't explain it, other than to tell you that it felt like he was inside me."[2]

The Arizal (Rabbi Isaac Luria, of blessed memory) explains in his mystical writings (recorded mainly by his great disciple Rabbi Chayim Vital, in *The Arizal*) that certain souls that have not arrived to their destined resting place are trapped mainly in the trees and vegetation. *Birkat Ha'ilanot* (the blessing recited in the month of Nisan on seeing the wondrous renewal in nature) helps to release these suffering souls and ease their travel to the final resting place.

Reciting this blessing is therefore considered a very great act of *chesed* for the whole of Israel. All the children of Israel are considered one; all our souls that were, are, and will be, come from the same place—from under the Throne of Glory of God. They are interlinked beyond the physical limits of body, time and space, as we know them. Just as the neshamot of the departed can intercede on our behalf "upstairs," so too should we help those souls who cannot be elevated without our help. The departed souls cannot fulfill any commandment, but we can.

The holy student of Rabbi Luria, Rabbi Gedalia HaLevi, used to tell his students that shortly after his death, he would return to this world. He also would stand every Friday on a hill just outside of Safed and see souls rising and descending from the cemetery (Rabbi Chaim Vital, *Sefer Hachezionot*, p. 40).

Angels

There are two kinds of angels that come into this world in order to perform a task—those that are seen by humans and those that are not (Zohar Bereisheet, Folio 34b). When they come down to Earth to perform a task in the presence of others, they appear like regular people (Zohar Vayera, Folio 101). The range of an angel's knowledge is limited to the task he is asked to perform and the information he is given. This is why at times he may not be able to distinguish between who is righteous and who isn't—if it is not relevant to the performance of his task, he will not be given any additional data. Nonetheless, they do have a broad view of the events that will take place in the future because they can hear God announcing His intentions throughout the various horizons (Zohar Vayera, Folio 102).

There are also angels of destruction who come down to this world. When man senses a dangerous situation, he should distance himself from it because he might otherwise get hurt. When an angel of destruction receives permission to act, he does not distinguish between those who are deserving and those who aren't. For example, when an angel is sent to cause damage to a specific area within a community, innocent bystanders could also get killed in the process.

During a funeral, the angel of death hovers among the women as they escort the deceased (from his house) to the cemetery and until they return to their homes. This angel can take away a person's life before his time because it reminds God of man's multiple sins. Therefore, men are warned to walk separately from the women while escorting the deceased—in this way, this angel will not have control over them. As a precaution, there are women who avoid going to the cemetery altogether (Zohar Vayakhel, Folio 196b).

Surprisingly, however, there are those who are immune to the

Angel of Death. It is said that whoever studies Torah will die at the hand of the Angel of Life. In this instance, the soul will connect to holiness and depart from its body with heavenly love—referred to as the kiss of death. The bodies of the righteous do not become impure upon death because since the Angel of Death has no power over it—not upon the soul's departure and not thereafter (Zohar Vayishlach, Folio 168).

Every angel has three animal-like images—an ox, eagle, and lion—and the face of man. Angels receive deserving souls with an abundance of pleasures (a more detailed description can be found in the Zohar Parshat Ekev, Folio 274). Here is a story of angels told to me by a parent who witnessed her child being escorted from this world to the next:

One day the sun was surrounded by a halo. It was in all the news reports. Nobody could explain it. I watched this phenomenon through the hospital windows. Tammy started to ask for the curtains to be closed at night—she sensed something out there, waiting for her. The third night she didn't ask—she was unconscious. I felt them coming. A few hours later, she was leaving with those invisible escorts. I heard a silent scream, not knowing what I was in fact hearing. I sensed the room filling with visitors, who could not be seen—a sensation of something grating. I watched as the body lay lifeless, and felt her going away, further and further with the visitors. She was gone, I was crying.

A while later, I was reading "Innerspace" (a book compiled from notes from Rabbi Aryeh Kaplan) and found the section describing how a cry goes forth when a someone leaves the world—announcing their passing. That at that time, there are *ophanim* (angels that go between worlds) present, and that there is friction when they pass.

I understood that indeed, I had been a part of my daughter's experience of leaving—we had been together, experiencing—she didn't have to do it alone. I really feel privileged to have been with her at that time (Rebbitzin Dr. Miriam Spalter, by personal communication—February 11, 2007).

Shaydim

There are three categories of *shaydim* (demons): those who reside under the Earth, where there are seven countries each with its own ruler; those who reside on Earth; and those who reside in the sky under the horizon.

Man sees only that which he can see with his eyes and has no cognizance of the fact that the atmosphere is filled with various beings of destruction (Zohar Bereisheet, Folio 55). From the moment one takes his first breath of air in this world, the evil inclination (*yetzer hara*) swoops down upon him. Hence one's soul serves man as his personal consultant for good counsel on how to be saved from the yetzer hara. A fascinating contrast is made here between man and animal. From the moment they are born, animals have a sense of what is dangerous and what is not. For example, animals will run away from fire. A human baby or toddler may actually crawl toward it, because the yetzer hara is in control. As adults, we also may tend to follow an urge that may not be in keeping with moral behavior. This, according to the Zohar, is when man must turn to and consult with his neshama (Zohar Vayeshev, Folio 179).

Sometimes a soul who misused opportunities in this world does not find peace, even after death. Such a soul might be denied entrance to gehinom and is not given the option to reincarnate, leaving it exposed to the mercy of demons and other spirits who compel it to wander aimlessly and helplessly. It desperately searches for a body to call its own, and when it does, takes possession of its faculties. This type of malicious, possessing demon is called a dybbuk (*Dybbuk*, pp. 286–287).

L'Chaim!

In days of old, wine would be given to a man about to be put to death to lessen his sorrow. Hence, today when we pour a glass of wine for someone, we say "to life!"

Death became a part of living after the sin of Adam and Eve. The Serpent was ensconced in impurity and so it entered the body of man. As a result, man's body has urges to seek impurities from time to time (some more than others), and therefore, with such a body it is not possible to reach the heights of spiritual bliss and maintain it, literally, forever. At Mount Sinai this impurity, stemming from the snake, ceased to exist. However, when the Israelites sinned with the golden calf, impurity was restored in man and death returned as a fact of life (Zohar Ki Tisa, Folio 194b).

Communicating with the Deceased

According to a survey conducted at http://www.beliefnet.com, 21 percent of respondents answered "yes" when asked if they had ever consulted a medium or psychic, 28 percent admitted to using a Ouija board, and 14 percent had participated in a séance. But the vast majority of those polled said they attempted to communicate with loved ones directly through prayer and meditation (63 percent) or by speaking to them aloud or in their minds (69 percent).

In a final question, "Have you ever felt as if a dead person was trying to communicate with you?" more than 3,800 people responded with testimonials detailing everything from the spirit of a dead cat appearing in a woman's lap to a deceased son giving his mother one last hug in a dream.

Unbeknownst to us, the back-and-forth travel of spiritual beings to their loved ones on Earth is going on night and day, all over the world. Dreams, a visitation beside one's bed that seems like a dream, visions of departed loved ones and appearances of religious figures, are all manifestations of a spirit's return. The major purpose of these visits is to guide those on Earth or to comfort those who are bereaved by a beloved one's passing. Souls from the other side are continually working to elevate the spirituality of those on Earth. By aiding in the spiritual growth of those on Earth, the attending spirit derives energies for its own advancement.

Another reason for a soul to return temporarily is to clear up some unfinished business. A recent occurrence in the Mea Shearim section of Jerusalem, as reported on a local news report, described this scenario:

A well-known rabbi passed away and a dog suddenly appeared in the courtyard of the house where the mourners were sitting *shiva*. He lay down close to the entrance of the apartment. This was a most unusual phenomenon, since dogs are almost never seen in this ultra-orthodox neighborhood. The residents of the area were both scared of the dog and bewildered as to why it had parked itself at the entrance to that particular apartment. Many attempts were made to chase the dog away, but all in vain. The dog wouldn't budge.

Finally, it occurred to one of the kabbalists in the area that perhaps this dog was a messenger of the deceased, and it was up to the family to take some kind of action. The rabbi explained this to the family, and apparently there was indeed some unfinished business between the deceased and his family. Subsequently, members of the family went to the grave, encircled it, and prayed for forgiveness. Shortly thereafter, the dog got up and left.

Souls seem to be able to choose to communicate with the living in various ways. But is it permissible to make a dying person swear to return to you after his death and answer whatever it is you want to ask?

My understanding is that forcing someone in this predicament to swear is not permissible. However, according to the Shulchan Aruch (14:179, 14), neshamot can and do return to this world in order to reveal some aspect of His glory to us.

Dr. Elisabeth Kubler-Ross, well-known for her seminal book *On Death and Dying* (1969), in which she explains her now classically regarded "five stages of grief," went to the funeral of Mrs. Weiss, a patient of hers. After the funeral, Dr. Kubler-Ross went to her office. Mrs. Weiss appeared in the office to thank the doctor for all she did for her. Kubler-Ross told Weiss that nobody would believe that this was happening, so she asked Mrs. Weiss to write something down on paper. Upon showing the handwriting to Weiss' family, they confirmed that it was indeed hers.

Another example of this kind of communication is told in *Sefer Hachezionot*. On his day of death, Rabbi Chaim Vital's father told his son not to be afraid of dying. If he wished to ask anything, he should feel free to come to the grave for an answer. And so it was that on a number of occasions, Rabbi Vital approached his father's grave to ask whatever was on his mind, and received an answer to every question (*Sefer Hachezionot*, p. 420).

Soul Reassignments

A living person consists of both body and soul. When the body dies, if the person merits it—a small portion of the soul remains with the body to keep it connected with the soul's source, anticipating the general revival of the dead at the time that God decrees. Different parts of the remainder of the soul may go to different places. One might be reincarnated into a new body in an attempt to perfect one of its spiritual shortcomings. One part might go to a level of paradise. Another might go to gehinom for a period to remove the sins of that life and prepare it for a future one. Another part might join temporarily with an already living person, to assist it with its rectification and, in the process, gather more merit. The reassignments of the soul continue until the time that God decrees its work is complete.

With regard to parallel lives, souls who choose to split between two or three bodies in the same lifetime do this in order to accelerate their learning. Generally speaking, Guides are against this splitting, but souls do have free will.

Another type of temporary travel that a soul does is similar to an NDE. A number of examples illustrate this:

A When the Israelites stood at Mount Sinai to receive the Torah and heard the first few commandments directly from God, they died out of fear, but were immediately revived by the same dew that will be used to resurrect the dead at Techiyat Hameitim (Tractate Shabbat 88b).

B In the story of Joseph, after Joseph put money in the sacks of his brothers, their souls departed for a moment out of fear and then returned (Genesis 42:28).

C There is also the well-known story of Elijah, who revived a boy who had lost his soul in the fields after the boy's mother came to plead for the prophet to revive him (Kings I, 17:17).

The Invisible World

Earlier we discussed the fact that the atmosphere is filled with beings. There are angels who accompany a person in all his travels, although he is not typically allowed to see or hear them (Zohar Mishpatim, Folio 116). Scientist Dr. Robert Crookall undertook a systematic study of hundreds of communications from the afterlife and published the results in his book *The Supreme Adventure* (1961). Crookall was amazed at the consistency of the evidence coming from all over the world. Communications from Brazil, England, South Africa, Tibet, Europe, India and Australia among others were all consistent. He found that they were identical with the beliefs held by the natives of the Hawaiian Islands, cut off from other civilizations for years prior to their discovery in 1788. He was also amazed at the consistency of the evidence given by people who had out-of-body experiences, NDEs, and communications through high-level mediums. Could such consistency be coincidental?

Imagine a world of its own that surrounds us—filled with people like us, souls without bodies floating around in the form of lights. All of these figures are coming and going. The traffic is heavy and there is always someone around. Intimidating-looking angels of destruction are out, especially at night, and those who walk or travel alone may be more prone to their evildoing. Having the accompaniment of at least one other person would protect one from these beings.

Naturally, since we cannot see them, we are less likely to be thinking about these beings, but I wonder whether an increased awareness of a populated plane directly above us would cause one to be more cautious before taking action. If you knew that somebody was watching your every move—even if you were alone in the privacy of your home or office—would that affect your decisions to follow through with certain actions? It would be more likely that someone in the presence of an audience would think twice about carrying out an embarrassing behavior. Unless one is wantonly brazen, an awareness of these spirits will compel us to put checks and balances on ourselves. Perhaps this line of thinking would prevent many of us from committing actions that we would otherwise regret taking.

The implications of this heightened awareness or mindfulness could certainly have far-reaching implications in our personal lives, altering our behaviors and belief systems to the core. Has your living room suddenly become more crowded?

CHAPTER SEVEN

Popular Questions and Answers

"In school, you're taught a lesson and then given a test. In life,
you're given a test that teaches you a lesson."

—Tom Bodett

Our Destiny

Was I put here on Earth in order to help someone else or were others put here to help me? Or were we both put here simultaneously to help each other?

Rabbi Gershon Winkler, author of *Dybbuk*, a psychological and philosophical study of the Jewish perspective on the odyssey of the human soul, says that everyone has his own purpose to realize in life. However, if one fails to achieve his own personal objective (whether by neglect or circumstance), he can elevate his soul by associating with or contributing to the fulfillment of another soul's purpose (*Dybbuk*, pp. 311–312).

An illustration of the concept of a soul coming down just to help another can be seen in the following example:

Twin girls were born into a family. One of the babies was born with leukemia and subsequently died at 15 months of age despite having had a good prognosis. A short while thereafter, the babies' father had a dream in which it was revealed to him by the deceased soul of his daughter that the only reason she came to this world was to accompany her sister, Yuval, who was afraid to descend to this world. She volunteered to come down for the short time it took for her sister to adjust to this world. The Hebrew name of the surviving twin, Yuval, more commonly given to a male, is translated as "was accompanied." We are taught that in naming their children, parents are given a certain spiritual insight. In this case, the name given to the surviving twin could not be more on target (Anonymous, by personal communication).

Spirit World Revisited

What is the spirit world like?
Clairvoyant people who have had glimpses into the world beyond say it is a world much like our own, but without time or space dimensions; it exists in a higher dimension of energy and in its higher realms is a world of inexpressible beauty. It is a world where it is possible to be fully alive, and where the whole body "perceives" its surroundings. It is a world of endless possibilities for creativity and full realization of self, and it is a world where the love of God is like the air we breathe. One's spiritual body can travel through thought waves, so that if one thinks of a person and place, he can immediately be transported there.

Communication is also accomplished by thought because one is free from the restrictions of the physical body. Even eating is not necessary to maintain the spiritual body. In the spiritual world, one realizes that life on Earth, like life in the womb, has been necessary preparation for a fuller, freer and richer eternal existence.

Preparing for Transition

What can we do while still living in our physical bodies to ease our transition at death?

We should educate ourselves as much as possible about the spirit world. Gaining even the smallest impression that there is life after death will bring enlightenment and understanding. The more one can illuminate the objective reality of the spirit world, the more one has the desire to live in accordance with natural and spiritual laws that enable us to go directly from Earth into the higher realms of the spirit world.

Seven Lands Beneath Earth

Are there other lands our souls may travel to?

Five different sources within the Zohar (Bereisheet 39b-40-40b, Bo 41b, Mishpatim 95, Vayikra 9b, and Zohar Chadash Bereisheet 8b) give slightly different accounts of the order and make-up of the lands in the afterlife, and their details don't exactly match up. Nonetheless, it is presented below for the reader to get a sense of the overall concept.

God created seven horizons above Earth and seven lands below Earth. In each of these horizons are stars and constellations, ministers, chariots, and angels comprised of six wings and four wings, some four-faced and some two-faced. Animals reside within set communities. Between each land there is a horizon that separates them and there are different living forms in each land.

There is a story told of Rabbi Nehorai (Zohar Vayikra, Folio 10) who sailed at sea and drowned due to a major storm that overturned his ship. Then a miracle happened—as he fell to the depths of the sea, he entered a land whereupon he saw people who were all small-sized, praying, but he didn't understand what they were saying. He was then brought straight up to this world where he testified to what he saw.

The Zohar details a number of lands, but there is no listing of the seven horizons alluded to above. Dwelling 6 may relate to what Newton's patients describe as the Space of Protection. The seven lands beneath Earth are described as such (in ascending order):

Dwelling 1 (*Eretz*): There is total darkness, no knowledge or form or existence. This place has no functional purpose. Tahariel is the angel in charge together with 70 others who fly in the atmosphere. After partaking in the apple from the Tree of Knowledge, Adam was chased from Gan Eden and arrived here on a Friday evening. He was bewildered but repented and thereby merited moving up to Adama on Saturday night.

Dwelling 2 (*Adama*): It is dark, but not entirely. Here exist sad and otherwise damage-causing life forms. The souls of Cain and Hevel were conceived here. Souls who died without bearing children on Earth are brought here to be judged. The angel Kedumiel is in charge.

Dwelling 3 (*Arka/Bohu*): There is light from the sun, and trees grow here, but there is no wheat. Life forms are born and also die. There are also sparks of fire and smoke, the continuation of the fire of *Na-har d'Nur*. Angels of destruction menace the wicked here.

Dwelling 4 (Gai): There is a vast territory here. Its length and width are explained in Tractate Pesachim 94. Gai is 1/60th of Gan, which is 1/60th of Eden, which is 1/60th of Gehinom. Light exists. Angels of mercy are seen and they do their specific task without revealing themselves to man. Padel is the minister. In this dwelling there are openings of mercy for those who return to God.

Dwelling 5 (*Neshia/Tohu*): Angels of judgment (who sing at midnight) and angels of mercy (who sing at dawn) exist here. Trees abound. Kadshiel is the angel in charge. There are life forms here similar to man but with short legs and two holes for a nose. The beings here are forgetful. Neshia means forgetfulness; hence, all of the Torah learned is forgotten.

Dwelling 6 (*Tzia*): Ships carrying angels from here sail the world to perform various tasks necessary in that world. Uriel is the minister. There is reference to the fact that this land may contain Gehinom. The land itself is described as very dry, with an atmosphere of high humidity. Faithful people reside here.

Dwelling 7 (*Tevel*): The highest land of all. This is Earth as we know it. There are no angels. This is the only land in which bread is eaten. All of the other lands described above have living forms that are similar to those of man in this dwelling.

Non-Believers

What happens to the soul of the non-believer?

The most common belief in contemporary traditional Jewish communities is that all souls proceed to the afterlife. Nearly all, barring a handful or two in all of human history, eventually end up in Gan Eden, even non-believers. However, the medieval Jewish thinker Maimonides opined that non-believers cease to exist upon death. His reasoning was that the ability to exist eternally is God's, and is only acquired by the soul to the extent that the soul knows of, and therefore shares some of the form of, God.

The Shechina, or God's presence, will appear to a soul in the same manner in which a soul appears before God. If the neshama prays frequently and learns Torah, then the Shechina knows that these elements are a permanent part of the soul. If, however, prayer and Torah are performed by a soul merely from time to time or by chance, then the Shechina will appear to the soul by chance (Reisheet Chochma, Shaar HaAhava, Chap. 6:78).

Recreation

What will we do in the spiritual world?

It depends on where we are in the spirit world. The higher realms of the spirit world are truly heaven; a world of enjoyment and recreation. People do things they enjoy, and keep company with people they enjoy. The skills, interests, and abilities developed on Earth may be reflected in the roles we choose in eternity. Each of us will contribute uniquely toward the goodness and beauty in our realm. Further, it is said that the spirit world is replete with transcendent beauty. Those dwelling in the higher realms are able to travel to its vast reaches.

The quality of life in the spirit world is directly affected by one's heart and activities on Earth. One grows spiritually by serving others with love. Thus relationships are very important.

We seek out relationships in this life that are comfortable, and the same is true in the spiritual world. We are likely to seek out our relatives, loved ones and ancestors. However, if there is a vast difference in spiritual development, a person of lesser development and thus having a lower "vibration," will be unable to enter a higher realm to which one of greater development has advanced. In this case, the more highly developed loved one may choose to visit a less advanced person in another world who is in need of spiritual development.

Rambam vs. Ramban

What is the disagreement between the Rambam (Maimonides) and the Ramban (Nachmanides) regarding what constitutes "the next world" (olam habba)?

In brief, the Rambam believes that at the Resurrection (Techiyat Hameitim), bodies will stand, eat and drink but will die again, with only their soul continuing on to olam habba. The Rambam's reasoning is that since eating, drinking and sex will not be necessary in olam habba, the body would serve no purpose.

The Ramban, on the other hand, believes that despite the fact that the body is diminished in its strength and there will be no eating or drinking in the next world, it nevertheless is an integral part of the soul and will not die. Rather, body and soul will enter olam habba together as one unit. The Ramban bases his opinions on Talmudic tractates that state death will be rescinded forever (Moed Katan 28b, Pesachim 68a, Sanhedrin 91b). He believes that this promise refers to the body as well.

Most of the kabbalists follow the opinion of the Ramban. According to this view, the body will become more spiritual in nature, more pure, and will be more subservient to the soul.

Olam Habba Defined

Does the "habba" in olam habba refer to the past (a world that already came), present (one that is about to come) or future (yet to come)?

The goodness that the righteous will receive has already been created—it is just hidden. Hence, "habba" is past tense because the next world was already created during the first six days of creation. God hid the goodness of the next world because the living creatures inhabiting Earth would not be able to withstand the intensity of its light in this world. Therefore, God utilizes one-seventh of its light in this world. The remaining light is saved for the next world (Shaar Hagmul L'HaRamban, pp. 461–463).

Dream Messages

How can we tell the difference between a plain dream and a prophecy? Why does God elect to deliver messages in dreams?

The prophet Jeremiah said (Jeremiah, Chap. 20) that the feeling one has during a prophecy is incredibly strong—as if one's heart is on fire. As to the second question, during sleep our physical powers wane and our intellectual powers wax. When one ages, the body decreases in strength, which is why we often see the elderly engage in more spiritual and ritual endeavors—they no longer run after physical urges and can therefore concentrate on getting closer to God (Nishmat Chaim, Article III: 5).

The Physically/Mentally Disabled

Why do the severely physically/mentally disabled often have a stronger spiritual perception than others?

When we see a person with severe physical and mental limitations, we might incorrectly assume that they are also limited in their understanding. The fact is that they all have *chochma* (wisdom); what they lack is data (knowledge) because of a glitch between their mind and body. The reason this population can "see" what other "normal" people cannot is because their bodies do not limit them. It is actually easier for the soul to function in a handicapped body, because it is not encumbered by its body's preoccupations. This explains, for example, how facilitated communication, a technique which allows people with little or no communication abilities to communicate with others at a level far exceeding their assumed skills, yields remarkable results with autistic children.

Somebody once lamented to me that his severely handicapped child will never walk nor talk, get dressed, feed or bathe himself. He asked me: "What good purpose is my son serving here? Why does he need to go through the torture and pain of having such a severe disability? Why does God put such beings on Earth altogether?"

The great twentieth-century rabbinic scholar, The Chazon Ish

(Rabbi Avraham Yeshaya Karelitz), was known to stand at attention when a mentally or physically challenged person entered the room. He explained that such individuals have special neshamot, or souls, and function on a much higher level than the rest of us. Their past lives were filled with Torah and mitzvot—they raised beautiful families, were brilliant students and were successful professionally. But these special neshamot begged Hashem to come back to Earth to make one or two little tikkunim toward perfection. For this reason they are born with severe disabilities; they have no further need to speak, hold a job or even do mitzvot. They are here in their seemingly limited capacities in order to give their parents and others around them the opportunity to do chesed. "Take care of me," they might say, "so that you can grow in your deeds. I am here to be an object of your love. Nothing more nothing less." Who are we, then, to judge whether their existence is justified?

The Chazon Ish stood for these individuals out of respect; they are a cut above—a special breed that should not be judged by their outer appearance.

Multiple Bodies for One Soul

When a soul is reincarnated several times, which body arises at the Resurrection with that soul? What becomes of the other bodies?

Rabbi Yosai answers that the last body to have done its tikkun on its entire three parts (nefesh, ruach, neshama) by virtue of performing mitzvot and having children will rise.

If the first body was preoccupied with the learning of Torah, and the reincarnated body only needed to do a small tikkun, then the soul would return to the first body to rise because the second body was only "on loan." The second body will also merit rising at the Resurrection, but will house only a small spark from the original soul (Zohar Pinchas, Folio 213).

A man who dies without children is grabbed by angels of destruction that pursue him in *kaf hakelah* (the Catapult) from place to place without rest until his brother saves him by marrying his deceased brother's wife and reviving his spirit in the child born of that union. Thus the deceased comes back into this world in the form of this baby.

So at Resurrection, which body rises? The body of the newborn? Yes. Then what happens to the spirit and body from which he was deceased?

The spirit which he left in his wife's body is temporarily stored in a rock behind Gan Eden and will join its original body at Resurrection.

Those who die without producing children will arise at Resurrection provided they performed mitzvot. For those who died without children by choice and refused to do mitzvot, God turns their bodies into other creatures, such as snakes, that will not arise at the Resurrection (Zohar Mishpatim, Folio 99b).

What happens to the body of the wicked who do not repent? As mentioned earlier, if he already incarnated a number of times, the last body that merited to do some sort of tikkun will rise at the Resurrection.

What happens to his previous bodies? They descend to Neshia (see fourth question above) where they exist and undergo repair— there are differences of opinion as to whether they remain there forever or eventually ascend to *Tevel*, our world. If during his first and second incarnations he did not repent, then his body is also lost, and the purpose of his existence in Neshia teaches us that there is no burial done in vain (according to Rabbi Beroka, a sage often visited by Elijah the Prophet). Rabbi Shimon, eminent disciple of Rabbi Akiva and author of the Zohar, believes otherwise—those bodies in Neshia will rise at the Resurrection after their repair by virtue of the righteous that descend to gehinom for the expressed purpose of bringing up souls who wanted to repent but could not accomplish their wish before dying. All agree that if one does not repent after a third incarnation, then the body remains in Neshia. Rabbi Shimon adds that even in the latter case, they will rise when God rebuilds and renews his world (Tikunei HaZohar, Folio 76).

Another view holds that only bodies in which souls manage to take root (or fulfill the law to perfection) are resurrected. Other bodies will dry up like trees and fall to dust (Waite, *The Holy Kabbalah*, p. 252). The Abarbanel (late fifteenth-century bible commentator) claims that only the first body in which a soul resided will rise—all the rest will not return.

Yet another theory is that the last body will arise and the previous ones will also arise but with new (different) souls.

Modern day Torah scholar Rabbi Moshe Armoni points out that souls implore the angel responsible for the Resurrection to place it in one of the bodies it previously had while living in this world. Since the soul bonds with the body that encases it, a different body will seem foreign and less worthy.

Importance of Torah Study

What special connection is there between Torah study in this world and its influence on the soul in the afterlife?

If we learn Torah in this life, after death we take a special path or road made up of Knowledge. Those who neglected study go astray in paths that lead to a region where they suffer punishment. The Torah accompanies the learned soul and defends him. For this soul, death is a non-issue—it will feel as if he slipped away into another time zone, like Elijah the Prophet and Chanoch—the only two biblical figures who didn't actually sustain a physical death. Each rose to heaven in the form he appeared on earth (Zohar Shlach, Folio 159).

Those dedicated to study in this world will also be occupied with it in the next world (Waite, *The Holy Kabbalah*, p. 246). The Torah is referred to as the tree of life. Metaphorically, one could say that there are those who hold the trunk of the tree, those who hold its branches, others who hold its leaves and yet others its roots (Zohar Miketz, Folio 193).

The Torah escorts man and watches over him so that strangers do not touch his grave and so that he does not get judged in *chibbut hakever*. Moreover, he will merit the ability to recall the Torah he learned when he rises at the Resurrection, when all will be revealed; he will also be among the first to rise.

For those who learned Torah at night, God adorns them in the morning with a string of chesed that will be recognized in both the upper and lower worlds (Zohar Shmini, Folio 36). In lower Gan Eden the Torah will speak to you like a good friend (Zohar Vayeshev, Folio 185).

The Zohar is full of references of how God chooses to come down to lower Gan Eden at chatzot (midnight) in order to partake in the pleasure of the learning of Torah with the righteous souls. As a side note, before God enters Gan Eden, he literally "beats the living daylights" out of the angels of destruction, saps them of their powers, and scatters them into the depths of an abyss (Zohar Terumah, Folio 130b).

CHAPTER EIGHT

Concluding Remarks

"If there's no chocolate in heaven, I'm not going!"
—*Anonymous*

I N THE LAST 35 years scientific research has been on the rise to investigate the mysteries that lie beyond this world. Dr. Sam Parnia of the University of Southampton is in the midst of a three-year research study to determine the scientific validity of near-death experiences (NDEs) and learn more about the nature of death and human consciousness. According to Parnia, who is also affili-ated with the Weill Cornell Medical Center in New York City, about 10 to 20 percent of hospital patients who experience cardiac arrest and are then successfully resuscitated report having been conscious to some degree when there was no heartbeat or oxygen reaching the brain. Many of these patients report elements of "typical" NDEs, including moving toward bright lights, meeting with relatives, and communing with spiritual beings. But some NDErs also claim to have witnessed events that occurred in the hospital rooms while doctors tried to resuscitate them, including details such as which instruments were used and even where their personal items were stored after they were pronounced dead.

At Imperial College Hospital's emergency room in London each of the stretchers has a pole with a plate attached to it at its top and on it is a picture known only to the physician who placed it there. One cannot see this picture from eye level—it can be seen only from high above. This same set-up exists in another 24 hospitals worldwide. Parnia's study, AWARE (AWAreness during REsuscitation), will investigate whether NDE patients are actually perceiving their environments in a state of unconsciousness. Many NDE patients report viewing hospital rooms from above, so visual cues have been placed in such a way that they are visible only from the ceiling. If patients are able to accurately describe any of these items, NDEs may gain scientific credibility. The data is expected to be released at the conclusion of the three-year study in 2013.

Reincarnation is already a science of sorts to many hynotherapists. Dr. Bruce Goldberg, author of *Past Lives, Future Lives Revealed* is a California clinical hypnotherapist who hypnotically "progresses" patients into their future lives. He explains reincarnation possibilities as follows:

Because there is no time or space on the other side, it is possible to incarnate at different times in our sense of history past, present, or future. The objective of reincarnation is simply to learn in this school called Earth. And you choose the time and place to best learn your lessons. Our Earthly series of lifetimes is certainly not the ultimate reality, but one of several possibilities. It is our mind, or consciousness, that continues through each one of our incarnations...We are in reality, energy. As such, we cannot be destroyed. We cannot die. We simply appear to change bodies every 75 years or so.

This very thought was echoed by Rabbi Menachem Schneerson (The Lubavitcher Rebbe). In their article entitled "What Happens After We Die," Rabbi Shlomo Yaffe and Yanki Tauber write that the Lubavitcher Rebbe would often point out that a basic law of physics (known as the First Law of Thermodynamics) is that no energy is ever "lost" or destroyed; it only assumes another form. If such is the case with physical energy, how much more so a spiritual entity such as the soul, whose existence is not limited by time, space, or any of the other delineators of the physical state. Certainly, the spiritual energy that in the human being is the source of sight and hearing, emotion and intellect, will and consciousness does not cease to exist merely because the physical body has ceased to function; rather, it passes from one form of existence (physical life as expressed and acted via the body) to a higher, exclusively spiritual form of existence.

Many of us are forced to think about existential questions like these only when we are confronted with a crisis. But every day things happen around us and to us for a specific purpose. Each person we come in contact with enters our lives for a reason. Some neshamot get replanted in this world to fix just one thing that they didn't accomplish in a previous life. They could spend 50 or 60 years living their lives waiting for that one critical moment that defines their whole purpose in being here.

Rabbi Yitzchok Kirzner once said that we (as physical beings) are given a soul in an underdeveloped state, and it is our task to develop that soul through its contact with the world. We create a relationship with our soul, and in doing so we create ourselves as expressions of it. By struggling to define ourselves in terms of the soul, we gain possession of it. Only by overcoming barriers placed in our path does the soul become something earned and thus our own. This, in the final analysis, is choice—our choice to pursue the knowledge implanted in our soul, or to suppress it.

Another way to develop the soul is through prayer. We stressed a number of times that prayer can be very powerful—enough to return a person to life. In heaven all kinds of calculations are formulated which are beyond our comprehension. The Zohar (Parshat Balak, Folios 204-206) relates a story about a young boy who cried profusely upon the death of his talmid-chacham-father Rav Yosi D'Pekiin. His prayers were accepted up in heaven and his father was revived, living an additional 22 years in order to educate his son. However, in return for these 22 years, another 13 individuals had to die in his stead. In another case (Ketubot 62b) Rav Chanina ben Chachinai left his home for 13 years in order to learn Torah. Upon his sudden return home his wife was startled and died of shock. The Rav prayed for mercy and she was revived.

God sees the whole picture from up above and formulates his calculations accordingly. We only get to see a piece of it. That is why we are often our own worst critics. Upon entering the spirit world we judge ourselves more harshly than God does. This is the kindness that God bestows upon us. He sees the entire landscape and only apportions relative values to each of our acts, weighing it all in the grand scheme of things.

Rabbi Zev Leff, author, community leader, and one of Israel's most popular English-speaking Torah educators once told the following story: In a public relations event for a local neighborhood supermarket, a contestant was selected among hundreds of candidates and given the opportunity to take home as many shopping carts filled with food and products as was possible within a span of 15 minutes. At the sound of the bell, the lady who was selected furiously charged up and down the various aisles to select the best and most expensive pieces of meat, wines, house wares and produce. After about eight minutes, she was beginning to show signs of fatigue and sweat poured down her face.

Imagine, if you will, somebody approaching her and suggesting that she sit down and take a rest in the middle of her shopping spree for three or four minutes. She would surely say he was crazy.

Can we really afford to rest on our laurels when we could be doing more mitzvot and elevating our status in the world to come? In essence, the fear of death moves man to seek closeness with his Creator.

In an essay entitled "Permission to Believe," Rabbi Marc Gellman, author of *Does God Have a Big Toe?*, writes:

> We all know that there is either something after death or there is nothing. Let us consider the possibility that there is nothing. Let us examine the possibility that death is the true and final end of us in every way—no heaven, no hell, no soul, no eternal life, no God. Just blackness and nothingness. Let us consider this charming, heartwarming, hope-inducing prospect...We have nothing to hope for beyond what we are capable of creating in the time allotted to us...In the final analysis all things crumble away into nothingness... ask yourself just one question: Can I live with this?

People who believe in olam habba (even if they have never heard the phrase or studied the texts that teach it) die with infinitely greater serenity than people who do not believe in the world to come. People who face a death conceived of as utter annihilation cannot be at peace—they are torn and bitter, and die in anger.

Gellman goes on to describe how he has seen dying women and men tell their deceased spouses that they were coming, and he knew that they were not speaking to nothingness. They were speaking to somebody.

Believing that death is not the utter extinction of those we love is the only hope strong enough to help us leave the gravesite and the only hope strong enough to help us cope with the cruelty of the world. However, this truth cannot be learned from a book or a professor or a theologian. It must be learned from life and from perhaps a rabbi, a parent or grandparent or friend—from someone who believes that it is true. And I believe that it is true. Any comfort I have ever been able to bring to the hearts of the sorrowing is driven and sustained by my faith in olam habba, which is essential and true, mysterious and wonderful, gentle and sure, challenging and comforting. We will be together again in that place. Turn right beyond the green pastures just beside the still waters, and you will find me. I will find you. I will be teaching Torah or golfing—one of the two—and you will say, 'How could we even have doubted that such a place was real?'

Glossary of Terms

Al Kiddush Hashem	Sanctification of God's name
Aliyat Haneshama	Ascendency of the Soul
Asiya	World of Action, the lowest of the four spiritual worlds described in kabala
Asseret harugei malchut	The ten martyrs
Atzilut	World of Emanation; the realm of pure divinity; the highest of the four spiritual worlds
Baalei Mishna	Talmudists of the oral law
Baalei teshuva	Those who repent and adopt a more observant lifestyle
Baal tzedakah	Philanthropist
Beit din	Court of Judges
Beit din elyon	Supreme Court

Bnei Noach	Those who follow the Noahide laws
Bracha	Blessing
Briyah	World of Creation, the second of the four celestial worlds; the world of the angels
Chai	Living animal
Chasidei Umot haolam	Righteous gentiles
Chatzer beit din	Courtyard of the court
Chavruta	Learning partner
Chayya	The part of the soul that allows one to have an awareness of the divine life force itself
Chayot hakodesh	Holy celestial beings
Chesed	Act of kindness
Chibbut Hakever	Pain of the grave
Cruvim	Angelic beings who support the throne of God and magnify His holiness
Derech	Path (of observance)
Dinar	A coin of worth
Domem	Inanimate object
Ein sof	Infinite
Erva	Nakedness
Gan Eden	Paradise
Gehenna (Gehinom)	Hell, purgatory
Gemara	The Talmud
Gevura	Might, power
Gilgul	Incarnation
Hakafot	Encirclement (with the scrolls of the Torah)
Hashem	God
Hasidim	Pious Jews

Heichalot	Temples
Hoshana Rabba	The seventh day of the Jewish holiday of Sukkot, 21st day of the Hebrew month of Tishrei; this day of "great supplication" is marked by a special synagogue service in which seven circuits are made by the worshippers with their *lulav* and *etrog*
Kabala	Torah mysticism
Kaf Hakelah	Catapult
Karet	The cutting of the soul, causing premature death on the earthly plane and a severing of the soul's connection with God on the spiritual plane
Kaddish	Prayer for the dead
Kaylim	Vessels
Kedusha	Holiness
Kever	Grave
Kiddush	Prayer preceding the blessing over wine
Klipot, klipa	A corrupt and loathsome (or foreign) shell
Lashon hara	Slander, gossip
Levushim	Garb, attire
Lower Gan Eden	The part of Paradise that a soul first reaches—he is encompassed by emotional bliss
Malachei sharet	Ministering angels
Mashiach	Messiah
Medaber	Term for a human
Mishnah	Collection of oral laws compiled by Rabbi Judah Hanasi which forms the basis of the Talmud

Mitzvot	Good deeds
Mochin	The mind (plural form)
Moed bet	Slang for a second chance
Nachat	Comfort
Nahar d'Nur	River of fire
Nefesh	Raw material of a soul that enters the body at birth; determines one's physical and psychological make
Neshama	A spiritual intelligence separate from the body; most elevated part of the soul
Neshama Kedosha	A holy or righteous soul
Neshama Yeteira	An "additional" soul that enters one's body on the Sabbath due to the heightened spirituality that engulfs the day; it could come in the form of elevated thoughts
Nidda	Status of a woman during her period of menstruation plus seven days thereafter
Ofanim	Type of angels
Olam Habbah	World to Come
Olam Hazeh	This world
Olam HaMalachim	World of angels
Olam HaNeshamot	Sanctuary of souls; located in Upper Gan Eden
Orot	Lights
Otzar haneshamot	Treasury of souls, world of souls (Also see: Olam HaNeshamot)
Pasuk	Verse
Pinkas	Notebook
Ratzon	Grace, favor

Rosh Chodesh	The first day of the new month
Rosh yeshiva	Headmaster of a Talmudic college
Ruach	Spirit; part of the soul that distinguishes between good and evil
Sfira, sfirot	Emanations of light from the upper world
Sefira Bina	A channel of Divine energy or life-force
Shiva	Seven days of mourning following a relative's death
Seir laazazel	Goat sent off to the wilderness for atonement to God (see Leviticus 16:10)
Seraphim	Type of angels
Shaydim	Evil spirits; demons
Shechina	Divine presence
Shema	A central prayer proclaiming the Oneness of God
Shemirat Haloshon	Careful speech
Shiur	Torah-based lesson or lecture
Shiva	House of mourning
Shofar	Ram's horn
Talmid chacham	Talmudic scholar
Tannaim	Scholars of the Mishnah
Techiyat hameitim	Resurrection
Tefach	Handsbreadth
Tefillin	Phylacteries
Teshuva	Repentence
Tiferet	Beauty, adornment; it is the balance between chesed and gevura, and the seat of compassion
Tikkun	Reforming, mending
Tikkun hamidot	The recognition of whether we were

	successful in understanding what aspects of our character needed to undergo "repair" in this lifetime
Tipah	Driblet
Torah	The five books of Moses
Tsror Hachayyim	Divine treasury of souls; "Bundle of life"
Tzaddik(im)	Righteous person(s)
Tzelem	Shadow, image, semblance, form, likeness
Tzelamim	Images, forms
Tzizit	Four-cornered garment with fringes
Tzomeach	Vegetation, plant-like
Upper Gan Eden	The supernal realms of Paradise
Yechidah	The highest plane of the soul that allows for full union with God
Yesh	Material or corporeal existence
Yeshiva	Sanctuary of Torah learning
Yetzer Hatov	Good inclination
Yetzer Harah	Evil inclination
Yetzirah	World of Formation, the third level of the four celestial worlds
Yisurin	Suffering, affliction
Yom Tov	Holiday
Yom Kippur	Day of Atonement
Zohar	Literally "splendor"; the book forming the basis of Kabala, authored by Shimon Bar Yochai (80–160 CE)

Endnotes

Chapter 3: The Soul's Journey on Earth, and Beyond

1   Lloyd Glenn, http://www.snopes.com/glurge/birdies.asp—1994.
    There are conflicting opinions as to the original source of this story;
    nevertheless it is a powerful illustration of the subject at hand.

2   Another opinion proposes that the primary personality of the soul
    will be the one that rises during the Resurrection. This latter opinion
    is somewhat problematic to envision on a practical level because it
    leaves us with an open-ended question: What does primary person-
    ality mean and how does that one element manifest itself exactly?

3   From a mineral to a vegetable state, transmigration takes place during
    the Hebrew months of Av, Elul, Tishrei and Cheshvan (correspond-
    ing to August, September, October and November). From a vegetable
    to an animal state—transmigration takes place during the Hebrew
    months of Nisan, Iyar, Sivan, and Tammuz (corresponding to April,

May, June, and July). From an animal to the articulate state—transmigration occurs during the Hebrew months of Kislev, Tevet, Shevat, and Adar (corresponding to December, January, February, and March) (Shaar Hagilgulim, Introduction 22).

4   Additional insight on this topic will also be explained in Step 46 on the Resurrection. For those who wish to read the detailed summary (in Hebrew) of the number of times we incarnate with special regard to varied circumstances of the righteous and the wicked, turn to *Tikunei HaZohar, Matok Midvash* commentary on Folio 76b, corresponding to Volume 20, p. 495.

Chapter 4: Inside the Map: A Detailed Tour

1   This announcement is heard in no less than 270 worlds. Not all announcements from above are heard in this world due to the thickness of the atmosphere, therefore God sends birds to fly around and literally "cut" the air to divide it up in a manner that the announcement can find holes in the thickness.

2   According to Rav Eliyahu DeVidash, at the moment of the announcement, a flame comes from the north and and kicks the wings of a black rooster. The rooster calls out three times with verses that awaken our judgment.

3   Hoshana Rabbah, or The Great Salvation, is a climactic day of praise to God that was also viewed by rabbinic authorities as a mini Day of Atonement, the day on which the heavenly decrees made on Rosh Hashana and sealed on Yom Kippur were actually sent out to be fulfilled.

4   There are six things that the Angel of Death commanded to Rabbi Yehoshua ben Levi. One of them was that when he enters the room of a sick person on his deathbed, not to stand at the person's head because there sits the *Shechina*, nor to stand at the person's feet be-

cause the Angel of Death is standing there with a sword in hand, etc. (Shaar Chupat Eliyahu, Chap. 6:10).

5 These levels denote the spiritual level that man achieved in his lifetime. For example, Palace #2 contains souls who have suffered morally and physically in this world but have nevertheless given daily thanks to the Almighty and have not neglected prayer. Palace #5 contains souls who submitted their lives for the sanctification of His name. Souls who have reached a certain level in life do not pass through the palaces below that grade, while those who are below work upward and attain that level after a given period in olam habba (Waite, *The Holy Kabbalah*, p. 249).

6 *"V'harav yotzei likrat hatalmid b'moto"*: Tractates Eruvin 54a, Nidah 37a, Sotah Yerushalmi 5:6.

7 For the wicked, the *Shechina* departs and Angels of Destruction come and proclaim "There is no peace to the wicked." The soul of the wicked leaves its body in a painful manner, as described in Brachot 8a, "kifturei b'fee veshet."

8 Kiss of death, as noted in Brachot 8b.

9 The physical plane (the world around us, our conscious reality) is composed of comparatively dense, slowly vibrating matter. The astral planes are generally divided into the lower, middle, and higher, although each division is actually said to contain many, many dimensions of varying vibration. When we shed our physical body, most of us reportedly wake up in our astral body living in the specific astral plane in which substance is vibrating at the same rate as the substance of our astral body. During our lives on earth and beyond, we apparently determine our vibratory rate by our thoughts, attitudes and spiritual understanding. Fear and resentment produce low vibrations, while love produces very high vibrations. Awareness of interdimensional realities produces high vibrations, while closed-

mindedness (whether religious, scientific, or political) produces low vibrations. Attachment to worldly things creates low vibrations, while calm detachment produces high vibrations. The lower astral planes are described as a dark, dismal world reminiscent of the Christian purgatory or hell. Some people of low-vibration thoughts and attitudes, after dying, are apparently pulled toward and trapped near the physical plane in a state of confusion. Without gravity or any sense of time or space in the spirit world, they might reside in this bewildering reality for years or for centuries of Earth time, not even aware they have died. The middle astral planes are described as a pleasant realm where most of us wake up to be rehabilitated after our earthly education in the school of hard knocks. The higher astral planes are apparently a wonderful, heavenly realm (Mark Macy, *Instrumental Contact with the Dead*).

10   The discarnate piece left behind in the afterworld is less communicative now, hence the dimmer light, but it is still capable of greeting a returning soul, albeit in a more quiet fashion.

11   See pp. 394–400.

12   http://Interfaithforums.com, June 2005.

13   Maharal in Tiferet Yisroel, end of Chapter 18.

14   http://www.shamash.org/lists/scj-faq/html/faq/12-08.html.

15   Those who engage in charity and chesed are immune to these spirits.

16   Interestingly, God showed Adam the entire book of the world's descendents—he saw all of the souls that will come down to this world—because Adam's soul is the source of their destinies. In addition, when Adam was in Gan Eden, God brought him a book via Raziel the Angel, Adam's mentor and the minister of the highest secrets. All of the angels wanted to know what was written in this book but God said to put it in geniza, hiding. After Adam sinned, the book was taken from him, and upon repenting he received only part of

it back, passing it along to his son Seth and through him to Avraham and finally to Hanoch, who gazed upon the uppermost echelons of the world and therefore left this world while still alive (Zohar Bereisheet, Folio 55b—see Matok Midvash, p. 665).

17 For a more detailed explanation on this, see Maavar Yabok, Siftei Renanot Chapter 35.

18 Rav Paalim, also known as The Ben Ish Chai, is Rabbi Joseph Chaim ben Elijah al-Chakam. Born in Baghdad circa 1835, he was a popular preacher, and his sermons were attended by thousands of people. Al-Chakam wrote many works, about both halachah and Kabbalah. One of these books, *Ben Ish Chai*, is a brief summary of practical halacha (comparable to the Kitzur Shulchan Aruch popular among Ashkenazic Jews), and remains very popular among Sephardic Jews to this day. He died in 1909.

19 J.D. Eisenstein, Otzar Yisrael; Rabbi Zalman Schacter Shalomi essay "Life in the hereafter: A tour of what's to come."

20 The ensuing description of what the Rabbi saw (fabulous temples) and what he learned (that saying the *kriat shmah* prayer which proclaims the oneness of God, will gain man entry to these temples) can be referenced in all its detail in Zohar Chadash Vol. III Midrash Ruth, beginning on Folio 109b.

21 As opposed to what the Zohar Chadash writes in Bereisheet Folio 27, that God creates this pillar when He wishes to ascend a soul.

22 As an experiment, I went with an escort (an esteemed and holy Rabbi) to one of the local cemeteries in Jerusalem approximately 90 minutes after Shabbat on January 31, 2009. We came equipped with flashlights and slowly, with reverence, we made our way between the rows of graves. We remained silent looking for any sign or hint of an image. My personal expectations were not high because I don't consider myself worthy of such visions, and I certainly didn't remember

receiving any sort of permission. My escort, however, stood a much better chance for meriting seeing these images, so I thought I could latch on and perhaps, from a distance, catch a glimpse of what may appear to him. Unfortunately, after about 30 minutes, we still didn't notice anything in particular and left in disappointment.

23 If it were not for Adam's sin of partaking of the fruit of Gan Eden, which brought major imperfections into this world, the soul could have continued its role in purifying the body without having to sustain a hiatus due to bodily death. Even the righteous Binyomin, Amram and Yishai, whose behaviors in this world were entirely meritorious, still needed to die in order to purify themselves. Despite all of their good deeds, it wasn't enough to wash away the stains that took hold as a result of the beguiling snake (Luzzatto, *Daat Tevunot*, p. 56)

24 http://www.sichosinenglish.org/books/to-live-and-live-again/04.htm.

Chapter 5: Olam Habba: The Order of Things in the World to Come

1 Sanhedrin 97a: Avoda Zara 9a. The Talmud speaks of five levels of man's ascension in spirituality. In the first 6,000 years man will worship God, in the seventh millennium he will be preparing for the new world, in the new world of the eigth millennium it is said that man will be pure and spiritual and the body will be subservient to the soul whereupon both can receive spiritual merits. In the ninth millennium the body becomes even more subservient to the soul and in the tenth millennium it will be totally subservient, a concept that is difficult for us in the current millennium to fathom.

2 http://www.sichosinenglish.org/books/to-live-and-live-again/04.htm. This is called the revelation of the *Ein-Sof* (infinite) light in this world. This involves the transformation of *yesh* ("there exists"), i.e., material and corporeal existence, into *ayin* ("nothingness"). This

elective self-nullification in the face of God's will allows His infinite light to become manifest in this world. The Torah and its commandments were given in this world to a soul garbed in a physical body so that the bodily and worldly yesh should be transformed into ayin and thereby become a self-effacing receptacle for the light of Divinity. Because the revelation of this light in the world is the purpose for which the world was created, it is clear that the intensity of this revelation will depend on the extent to which man elevates the physical world. For those souls who still were not able to accomplish a total *tikkun*, it may be that all will rise from their respective graves during *Techiyat hameitim*, however not all will necessarily derive the ultimate pleasure from the aura of the *Shechina*. The Zohar (*Parshat Chaye Sarah*) elaborates on the topic of Techiyat hameitim for those interested in a more in-depth look at the worthiness of souls who arise at that time.

3   Chabad.org Ideas and Beliefs—Y. Tauber and Rabbi Shlomo Yaffe.

Chapter 6: Connections Between This World and the Next

1   This story was related to me by a friend of a friend who claims its reference is from an article in a family magazine from a few years ago but could not backtrack to its exact source.

2   (http://www.highbeam.com/publications/Chicago-sun-times-p392330/aug-22-2007).

Bibliography

Adler, Jerry (2007, July 23). Back from the Dead. *Newsweek Magazine.*

Armoni, Moshe (2008). *K'Gan Raveh.* Jerusalem: Nachalat Rachel Publishing.

Azulai, Mordechai (1685). *Chesed L'Avraham.* Amsterdam: Attias Press.
Revised edition printed in 1996, Jerusalem: Machon Shaare Ziv.

Ben-Israel, Menashe (1656). *Nishmat Chaim.* Amsterdam.
Revised edition printed in 1995, Jerusalem: Yerid Hasfarim.

Ben-Nun, Yoel (1988). Nationalism, Humanity, and Knesset Yisrael. *In:* Ish Shalom, Benjamin and Rosenberg, Shalom, eds. *The World of Rav Kook's Thought.* New York: Avi Chai.

Ben-Shlomo Zalman, Eliyahu (The Vilna Gaon) (1873). *Even Shlayma.* Vilna: S. Mahltzon. Revised edition printed in 1987, Jerusalem: Yofi Publishers.

Brachia, Aharon (1896). *Maavar Yabok.* Vilna: Ram Press.

Cohen, Zamir (2006). *The Revolution. Science Reveals the Truth in the Bible* (Hebrew). Jerusalem: Hidabroot Press.

Cohen, Zamir (2010, Sept. 7). Lecture on "Life After Death" [Online]. www.hidabroot.org.

Cousins, Norman (1979). *Anatomy of an Illness.* New York: W.W. Norton.

Danzig, Yitzchak (1890). *Stories from the World of Truth* (Hebrew). St. Petersburg, Russia: V. Ettinger.

De Vidash, Eliyahu (1708). *Reisheet Chochma* (Hebrew). Amsterdam: Amsterdam Press. Revised edition printed in 2000, Jerusalem: Chaim Yosef Waldman, Machon Ohr Hamussar.

Doore, Gary (1990). *What Survives?* Los Angeles: Tarcher.

Ftaya, Yehuda (1933). *Minchat Yehuda.* Baghdad: Self-published. Sixth edition printed in 1990, Jerusalem: Machon Ftaya.

Ginsburgh, Yitzchak (2004). *Body, Mind and Soul.* Jerusalem: Gal Einai Institute.

Goldberg, Bruce (2004). *Past Lives Future Lives Revealed.* Franklin Lakes, NJ: New Page Books.

Groopman, Jerome (2004). *The Anatomy of Hope.* New York: Random House.

HaLevi, Rabbi Chaim David (1978). *Aseh Lecha Rav.* Jerusalem: HD Publishing.

Hechasid, Yehuda (1992). *Sefer Chasidim.* Jerusalem: Aharon Bloom Publishing.

Hyde, Catherine Ryan (1999). *Pay It Forward.* New York: Simon & Schuster.

James, John W. and Friedman, Russell (2004). *The Grief Recovery Handbook.* Sherman Oaks, CA: The Grief Recovery Institute.

Kaplan, Aryeh (1982). *Meditation and Kabbalah.* York, ME: S. Weiser.

Kaplan, Aryeh (1997). *Sefer Yetzirah* (The Book of Creation). Revised Edition. York, ME: Weiser Books.

Kastner, Bernie (2007). *Understanding the Afterlife in This Life.* Jerusalem: Devora Publishing.

Klapholtz, Yisrael Yaakov (1989). *The Jewish Soul* (Hebrew). Bnai Brak: Mishor Publishing.

Lamm, Maurice (2004). *Consolation.* Philadelphia: The Jewish Publication Society.

Livkin, Yisrael (1890). *Ohr Yisrael*. Vilna. Editor: Rabbi Yitzchok Blazer. Revised edition printed in 2005: Jerusalem: Feldheim Publishers.

Luria, Isaac (16th century). *Shaar HaGilgulim*. Tzefat. Revised edition printed in 2003, Jerusalem: Ahavat Shalom Publishing.

Luria, Isaac (16th century). *Shaar Hakavanot*. Tzefat.

Luzzato, Moshe Chaim (c. 1745). *The Way of God*. Amsterdam. Corrected edition printed in 1998, Jerusalem: Feldheim Publishers.

Luzzato, Moshe Chaim (c. 1740). *Daat Tvunot*. Amsterdam. Revised edition printed in 1982, Jerusalem: Feldheim Publishers .

Maimonides (Moses ben Maimon) (1702). *Mishne Torah*. Hilchot Teshuva, Chap. 8; Yesodei HaTorah, Chap. 4. Amsterdam edition. Original compiled between 1170–1180 in Egypt.

Miller, Avigdor (1973). *Sing, You Righteous*. New York: Balshon Printing.

Morse, Melvin (1992). *Transformed by the Light*. New York: Ballantine Books.

Nachmanides (13th century). *Shaar Hagmul*. Early editions were printed in Warsaw, and then in Constantinople in the year 1519. Revised edition printed in 2005 by Rabbi Yoel Sperka, Oak Park, MI: Oat Chaim.

Newton, Michael (1994). *Journey of Souls*. St. Paul, MN: Llewellyn Publications.

Newton, Michael (2000). *Destiny of Souls: New Case Studies of Life Between Lives*. St. Paul, MN: Llewellyn Publications.

Riemer, Jack (1995). *Wrestling With the Angel*. New York: Schocken Books.

Smith, Suzy (2000). *The Afterlife Codes: Searching for Evidence of the Survival of the Human Soul*. Charlottesville, VA: Hampton Roads.

Solomon, Lon (2005). *Brokenness: How God Redeems Pain and Suffering*. Potomac, MD: Red Door Press.

Sturzaker, Doreen and Sturzaker, James (1975). *Colour and the Kabbalah*. New York: Samuel Weiser.

Sunderland, Margot (2000). *Using Story Telling as a Therapeutic Tool With Children* (Hebrew). Jerusalem: Ach Publishing House.

Tatelbaum, Judy (1983). *The Courage to Grieve*. London: Cedar Books.

The Zohar (2003). New York: The Kabbalah Centre International. Original ancient text authored by Rabbi Shimon Bar-Yochai.

The Talmud: Tractate Chulin 142.

The Talmud – Midrashim: Tractate Gan Eden.

The Talmud: Tractate Kidushin 39.

The Talmud – Midrashim: Tractate Seder Gan Eden.

Tivon, Gil Gershon (2005). *Zoharic Secrets of the Soul* (Hebrew). Telz-Stone, Israel: Self-published.

Tsingel, Avraham (1985). *Stories from the World of Truth*. New York: Ben Adam.

Twerski, Abraham J. (1985). *Generation to Generation*. New York: Traditional Press.

Ullman, Rabbi Yirmiyahu (2006, Feb 4). *Soul Survivor* [Online]. http://ohr.edu/yhiy/article.php/2488.

Vital, Chaim (c. 1572). *Sefer Hachezionot*. Tzefat, Israel. Revised edition printed in 2002, Jerusalem: Shuvi Nafshi Press.

Waite, A.E. (1960). *The Holy Kabbalah*. New York: University Books.

What do Jews say happens when a person dies? Do Jews believe in reincarnation? In hell or heaven? Purgatory? [Online]. http://www.shamash.org/lists/scj-faq/HTML/faq/12-08.html.

Winkler, Gershon (1981). *Dybbuk*. New York: The Judaica Press.

Yaffe, Shlomo and Tauber, Yanki (2005, August 28). *What Happens After We Die?* [Online]. http://www.chabad.org/library/article_cdo/aid/282508/jewish/What-Happens-After-We-Die.htm.

Zohar (Matok Midvash commentary in Hebrew by Rabbi Daniel Frisch) (1986). Jerusalem: Matok Midvash Institute.

CDs

Armoni, Moshe (2009). *The Resurrection and Secrets of the Soul* (Hebrew). Jerusalem: Nachalat Rachel Organization.

Asharov, Yuval HaCohen (2012). *The Cycle of Life. Is Death the Beginning or End?* Merom: Tefillas Shai Organization.

Aiken, Lisa (1996) (Audio Tape). *How to Cope With Loss*. Jerusalem: Israel Center Library.

Chotam Emet (2011). Tiberias: Bechagvei Hasela Organization.

Clinical Death (Hebrew) (2009). Distributed by 03-950-4101.

Yaakov, Moshe (2009). *Yordei Hamerkava B'mearath Hamachpela in Hebron* (Hebrew). Produced in cooperation with Cable Channel 26 Raglei Mevaser, Israel.

Films

What Dreams May Come (1998). Dir. Vincent Ward. Universal.

Fearless (1993). Dir. Peter Weir. Warner Bros.

Defending Your Life (1991). Dir. Albert Brooks. Warner Bros.

Appendix

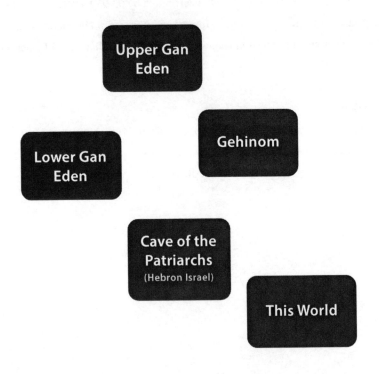

Figure 1: Juxtaposition of This World vs. Next World

Notes to Figure 1

1   The distance between lower Gan Eden and this world is one *tefach* (one handbreadth, according to Rav Acha). Rabbi Yochanan (Midrash Kohelet 7:12) says the thickness of a wall, and Rabbanan says the width of two fingers.

2   Lower Gan Eden is situated in the southwest vis-à-vis Gehinom in the north.

3   Upper Gan Eden is located in the horizon in olam habriya.

4   The Cave of the Patriarchs is the connecting point through which souls travel going from this world to lower Gan Eden. It is part of this world (looking at the above diagram it may seem as if it is situated northwest of this world) and is located about 19 miles to the south of Jerusalem, whereby Jerusalem is in the center of this world.

5   There is a pillar that connects lower Gan Eden to upper Gan Eden (not shown here).

6   There are seven heavens between upper and lower Gan Eden (not shown).

7   Earth is located more southeasterly.

8   The form of "this world" (olam hazeh) is in the shape of the letter "bet" (ב).

9   The reader should note that the above measurements and distances may not actually appear in relation to one another as described above since the terminology in the Zohar may be a spiritual reference and not a physically geographical one. For example, "north" may not be north as we know it. A "tefach" may appear differently than we have come to understand it to be.

The purpose of Figure 1 is to give the reader some sort of a picture of location relationships given the absence of exact coordinates.

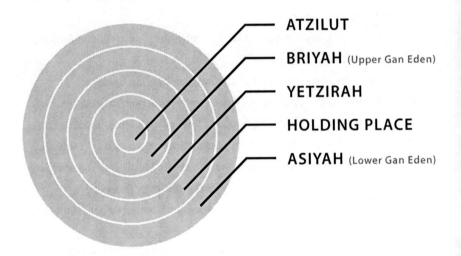

ATZILUT

BRIYAH (Upper Gan Eden)

YETZIRAH

HOLDING PLACE

ASIYAH (Lower Gan Eden)

Figure 2: Stages of Soul's Descent Before Entering This World

Acknowledgments

There are many people I would like to thank for their guidance, assistance, encouragement, good will, expertise and advocacy. Family first. Thank you to my wife Iva, my marriage partner of 33 years, for her encouragement and for allowing me the freedom to pour over the vast amount of texts and materials while she held down the fort. There aren't enough words of praise that will do justice to all Iva has done behind the scenes to gently prod and challenge me. She is a constant source of comfort and inspiration. Where would I be today without you?

To my mother, Hedy Kastner, and mother-in-law, Frances Korenblit, of blessed memory, my sincere gratitude for their constant support, in every sense of the word, and for making me feel the importance of the task I had undertaken. I especially appreciate them acting as informal publicists, recommending my first book to many of their friends and acquaintances. Likewise to my brother, Dr. Ron Kastner and his wife Dr. Elana Kastner, for their insightful feedback on a number of issues contained herein, and for generously donating my first book to those in need. Their actions pushed me to complete this book as quickly as possible.

Special thanks to my son Yaakov for his invaluable editorial input to the manuscript and for pointing out sections that needed extra clarification. Warm hugs and gratitude to my other children, Sara (and husband Doron), Zev Chaim, Chaviva, daughter-in-law Leiba, and grandchildren, who often had to endure my semi-lectures and offbeat views on certain family members I believe to be an incarnation of deceased relatives. To my beloved father Irving Kastner, of blessed memory, father-in-law Aron Korenblit, of blessed memory, and to our son and personal angel, Gedalia Natan, of blessed memory—who all left this world not too long ago and are sorely missed—you no doubt know the contents of this book from your personal experience, having had your souls make the journey from here to the exalted haven you enjoy today. I hope that I wasn't too far off in my descriptions here and, if I was, please come to me in a dream and tell me what revisions I need to make for its second printing!

Toward the outset of my journey I made a list of sources I would absolutely have to study in order to strengthen my knowledge of the subject. I thank my good friend and old college buddy Irwin Kotler for serving as the springboard. There were some very old books, some out of print, that were vital to my understanding, and therefore I am indebted to Yehuda Barkai for identifying, suggesting, gathering and then making available to me most of the Judaic texts I needed to have access to. Once I had these texts, I often consulted with a number of rabbinic authorities, and believe me, there were many. To HaRav Yaakov Hillel, the Rosh Yeshiva of Yeshivat Chevrat Ahavat

Shalom in Jerusalem, who encouraged me with cautious optimism in taking on this task and pointed out potential obstacles I might encounter in formulating my theories. I am indebted to him for recommending one of his shining students, Rabbi Mordechai Aran, an outstanding Torah scholar who would become available to me for guidance. It turned out that in his revered modesty, he suggested that I refer any questions on the Zoharic texts to another Torah scholar who he felt was better suited to answer my questions: Rabbi Yehuda Srevnik, Rosh Kollel of Yeshivat Tiferet Beit David, and the author of *Secrets of the Soul*. When the number of queries began to accumulate, I asked HaRav Srevnik if he had any time to learn with me. As the headmaster of an institute for higher Torah learning, he was with his students all day and evening at the *yeshiva*—the only time he had free was Tuesday nights between 10:30 pm and midnight. I gladly accepted. Over two years, I had the privilege of learning of the treasures of the Zohar together with him. With his vast knowledge of both Judaica and secular subjects and his ability to bring in vivid stories and examples, it made many a complex issue much easier to comprehend. He acted as my guiding light and put me at ease regarding doubts I had in making sense out of the many unfamiliar pieces of the puzzle I was grappling with.

Another dear friend I am grateful to is Rabbi Chaim Richman, one of the esteemed directors of The Temple Institute, a Torah scholar who learned with me at length and who often, with patience, took the time to walk with me on our way home from *shul* on many a *Shabbat* to discuss the subject matter. I especially appreciate his ability to put many challenging issues into perspective and for helping me keep the tone of the text on an even keel. Special thanks to him for referring me to Sam Peak, who took the time to enlighten me on a number of related themes in the book.

I also wish to extend a hearty thank you to another Torah scholar and a member of our congregation who also generously took time out of his busy teaching schedule to periodically learn with me at night, Rabbi Zadok Elias. I am particularly indebted to him for making me realize that there are no quick answers that can be handed to me on a silver platter. This forced me to have the discipline to sit and learn first-hand from the texts. Any reward I may have received from all those extra hours of learning is to his credit.

I would also like to thank a number of professionals who took the time to share experiences with me and exchange ideas. To Rabbi Efim Svirsky, an educator and therapist who enlightened me on past life regression, and to Minda Garr, formerly an academic advisor of the School of Social Work and Social Welfare of Hebrew University in Jerusalem for allowing me to have a glimpse into her specialized training in past life regression, especially as it relates to spiritual and therapeutic healing.

Thanks to Michael Cohen, a filmmaker, who expressed an interest in widening the potential audience of the book via a short film. Another key individual I am indebted to is Professor Joshua Ritchie, M.D., Dean of the Refuah Institute in Jerusalem, who was one of my dissertation advisors during the days of my original research while working on my doctorate. That dissertation led to the publication of my first book, *Understanding the Afterlife in This Life* (2007), and I want to take this opportunity to thank Professor Ritchie for his expert guidance in helping me construct the research methodology I utilized for testing and observing effective ways of overcoming the fear of death, the results of which I apply in my psychotherapy practice.

There were a number of CD and audio lectures provided to me by Rabbi Moshe Armoni, himself among the lecturers on the subject of the World to Come, that were incredibly useful. And special thanks to Rabbi Moshe Polin and Rabbi Yosef Carmel of Eretz Hemdah, an institute for advanced Jewish studies in Jerusalem, for answering a number of questions early on in my research for this book. I would also like to thank Rabbi Polin for inviting me to lecture at a meeting of the Rabbinical Council of America's Israel branch on the subject of Life After Death. The question and answer period that followed was quite enlightening.

By the time this book is published, another two books I authored (in Hebrew) will have already been printed and distributed. One is entitled *Masa El HaOr* (*Journey to the Light*), a children's book. The second is entitled *HaOlam She'Acharei* (*The Next World*). Since the material presented in both of those books is closely tied to the contents of this book, I would like to give sincere thanks to Dr. Oz Martin, a true friend and colleague, for the many heart to heart talks we've had related to spirituality, and for his writing the forewords for each book. Also thanks to his wife, Orit, co-author on the second Hebrew book, for suggesting the titles of both books. Likewise I wish to thank Professor Ben Corn, Head of Radiation Oncology at the Tel Aviv Sourasky Medical Center for his review of the children's text from a medical perspective and for his ongoing encouragement for me to continue writing, and to his wife Dvora, Executive Director of Life's Door-Tishkofet/Maagan, for including me over the course of a number of years as part of the psychotherapy staff of this organization that does a tremendous job in bringing hope and healing across the country and abroad to those suffering from serious illness. Having the opportunity to interact with the population they serve gave me further impetus to write on the subject of the afterlife in the hope that it will make a difference in the lives of those who embrace it.

I would be remiss if I didn't express my sincere appreciation to my book consultant Miriam Shaviv. From the raw manuscript, which I thought was ready for publication, to each successive draft and re-write, Miriam—your comments were always incisive and constructive and designed to make me sound better and more coherent. Your personal interest and regard for the contents of this book from our very first communication and thereafter were unparalleled—fortunately for me and for the readership. You have my heartfelt thanks and respect. And a special thank you to Rabbi Hanoch Teller for recommending Miriam to me.

Another special thanks goes to Willy Lindwer, documentary filmmaker and TV producer, and to Dr. Fred Kron, President of Medical Cyberworld, Inc. and former staff writer at Universal Studios and Disney Studios, who have separately taken of their time to help me think through how to take the written word from this book and turn it into an audio and visual apparatus that could one day be experienced by young and old alike.

Also special thanks to Willy Lindwer for introducing me to Rene van Praag, publisher of RVP Press. My sincere gratitude extends to Mr. van Praag for his vision and courage to take on this book project, whereupon other publishers (and there were quite a few) chose to opt out. And kudos to Astrid Bosch for her expert design of the book's contents and for her fine handling of other aspects of the book's production.

My gratitude to the Almighty, who provided me with the means and gave me the courage, strength and determination, to begin and complete this book, goes without saying.

Finally, to all those who shared fascinating and inspirational stories and the death-bed visions of loved ones (apologies to those that were not able to be included in this text); to all the well-wishers who read *Understanding the Afterlife in This Life* and took the time to give me feedback; to my good friend Dr. George Goldberg, a seasoned physician and musician, for his overall feedback and acting as a sounding board for me; to my long-time *chevruta* (study-partner) Yaakov Straus, who enthusiastically tackled many texts and sources together with me and provided much-needed clarity; to friends and colleagues who sent me clips and articles of interest; and especially to those who expressed a bit of anxiety and genuine disappointment each time I responded that I needed "just a little more time" to complete the book—to all of you, collectively and individually, may God bless you and grant you much health, happiness and success... and the time to enjoy them all.

Bernie Kastner
October 2013
Jerusalem, Israel

Lightning Source UK Ltd.
Milton Keynes UK
UKOW05f1007100614

233150UK00017B/791/P